Live the Life God
Envisioned for You

IMMERSION

Mark McNees

Triumph
Media

Free downloads of Pro Presenter® & Power Point® slides, message outlines, series graphics, *Immersion* banners, pre-message into video, immersion messages, "Group Swims" (Bible Studies), and W.H.O.L.E. worksheets are available at www.immersion4groups.com for anyone who wishes to use *Immersion* to promote The Gospel of Jesus Christ.

All Scripture quotations, unless otherwise indicated, are taken from the Tyndale House Publishers. (2004). Holy Bible : New Living Translation. (2nd ed). Wheaton, Ill.: Tyndale House Publishers.

Cover Image: Copyright: Schmid Christophe Image ID: 17370553 Release information: Signed model release filed with Shutterstock Images LLC

Cover Design: Mark McNees

Picture of Mark McNees on back cover was taken by Ashley Poole www.apoolephoto.com

Some of the stories are compellations with some of the details changed to protect the identities of the people involved.

ISBN-13: 978-1460967706
ISBN-10: 1460967704

Dedication

I would like to dedicate this book to my Mum and Dad
who never gave up on me.

CONTENTS

Acknowledgments

Writing this book has been one of the hardest things I have ever done in my life and there is no way it could have been completed without the help, input, and longsuffering of many people.

I would like to thank,

- **John Bickley** for meeting with me every Friday over coffee for months to hash out all these ideas and help organize them into a coherent book. It would not have happened without you.
- **Bruce and Karen Bickley** For the final edits and encouragement.
- **Rene' Meyer** for putting her professional touches on the cover.
- **Ashley Poole** (www.apoolephoto.com) for my picture.
- **Nicole Dunaetz** for fleshing out the metaphor with me.
- My wife **Shannon** and kids, (**Madison** and **Eric**) who encouraged me along the way. I would also like to apologize to my daughter, because apparently this book makes her sneeze.
- **Rebekah Abbot, Judy Abbot, Rebecca White, Amanda Matthews**, and **Theresa Bogema** for reading my blog and helping me refine many of these ideas.
- **Element3 Church** for being so supportive and blessing me with so many experiences.
- **Linda Clare** who encouraged me along the way and offered so much constructive insight in the development of *Immersion*.

The ideas in this book derive from years of sitting under great teaching and reading amazing books. I tried to credit everyone for their contribution to this book, but I am sure I missed someone.

Forward

Every Friday morning it would be waiting for me in my inbox. Another automated email reminding me of my 1pm editing session at the coffee bar with Mark. It became our Friday ritual. Meet for an hour or two and read through the new pages Mark had written that week.

What started off as a seven-chapter book became a seven-section book. Chapters grew and divided, were reimagined and relocated. The fitful joys of the recursive process of writing. The surprising journey of a book's natural growth.

Eventually, we racked in about six months of Fridays – yet somehow our Friday meetings never grew old or tedious. Quite the contrary, in fact. Our Friday sessions gained momentum as they clicked by. Counterintuitively, they grew more fresh, more engaging, more... new.

The secret to this increased feeling of newness was of course the Gospel. For a literature guy like myself, it is a storyteller's paradox: The more one hears the story of Jesus, the more new it becomes. Of all the pastors I have met, Mark understands this truth, lives in this truth the best.

I did not fully comprehend it the second time I attended Element3 Church (E3), but I had returned to that untraditional gathering space to witness and experience a very specific thing. The "new." Not the newest worship set or "unchurchy" postmodern atmosphere; I recognized instead the perpetual newness of a life in Jesus. While I've never heard Mark say it quite that way, and the church's statement of beliefs does not spell it out in so many words, the ethos of E3 is the newness of a life immersed in God's grace.

Those who attend the Sunday worship gatherings at E3 experience this every week in Mark's teachings. Not perfection or spiritual transcendence; rather, a life of authentic faith, made new every morning. The reality of our daily walk with Jesus: our love ever a first love, our hope again restored, faith ever renewed.

Mark's authentic approach to the realities of living out this rich and satisfying life of faith is geared to meeting people where they are. His perspective on the message of God finds its pages always fresh, its teachings and stories always immediate and personal.

This book is an organic outgrowth of this renewing walk of faith. It looks anew at the redemptive love of Jesus and His greatest charge to His followers, loving Him holistically and loving others as ourselves. It is a personal letter, an encouragement, and a challenge to experience a life immersed in the grace of God.

John Bickley

Introduction

I would like to thank you for taking the time to read *Immersion*. It is my prayer that this book will be a blessing and an encouragement to you in your journey as a fellow follower of Christ. I also pray that it will assist you in experiencing the rich and satisfying life Jesus came to give His followers, and that, in the process of reading this book, you will make The Great Commandment the primary grid through which you make all your life decisions.

I have done my best to directly connect the ideas in this book to scriptural passages. Footnotes and textual citations are included on the same page for easy reference and further contextual study.

The book has been organized into seven parts. Part one sets the stage for the five central sections. A seventh and final section is intended as a "putting it all together" framing piece.

I have also written a group study which is located at the end of each section, with the hope that you will go through this book in community. You can do the studies alone, but everything is better in community.

In the back of the book there is a 40-day life coaching experience, designed to help you experience a richer and more satisfying life. There are also free resources for your church and small group Bible studies available at:

www.immersion4groups.com

The greatest blessing to me would be that the body of Christ would be encouraged, equipped, and edified as people join together in their homes for elevated conversations. These group studies are intended to facilitate just such conversations.

In His Grip,
Mark

part 1
Life Immersed
the great commandment

chapter one

ESCAPE 2009

> "To do anything in this world worth doing, we must not stand back shivering and thinking of the cold and danger, but jump in, and scramble through as well as we can."
>
> -Sydney Smith (1771 - 1845)

I balanced on the edge of the ferry, my hand gripping the rail, my eyes scanning the choppy waters of San Francisco Bay, and thought, *Maybe this wasn't such a great idea....*

The frigid air made me appreciate my fellow competitors packed in beside me on the ferry; it somehow made what I was about to do seem a little more sane. There was a collective inaudible hum of thoughts processing the looming leap into the inhospitable water. As I watched some choose not to make the leap after all, I too asked myself again if I really wanted to follow through with this increasingly irrational decision. Did I want to do what the California prison system said could not be done? Did I really want to attempt this "Escape from Alcatraz"?

"Escape from Alcatraz" is an annual triathlon held every summer. The race begins with the most daunting task first, the swim from Alcatraz Island to the shores of San Francisco. This uniquely demanding race admits only 2000 athletes from as many as 40 different countries, all converging on San Francisco with one goal in mind: to break out of "The Rock."

The day before the race, I had the opportunity to take a tour of the island. As I walked the halls of the prison and read the stories of those who were incarcerated there, I felt the oppressive air of the concrete and steel, built to keep a relentless grasp on its inhabitants, to choke out all dreams of a better future. Hope and beauty and anticipation of tomorrow were locked out by its 50' barbwire-topped walls and intricate fail-safes, all surrounded by the freezing cold waters of San Francisco Bay.

SWIM TO FREEDOM

So, there I was, willingly ferried out to do what wardens and inmates and politicians alike thought was not possible. As we expected – yet still somehow unthinkably – the race officials instructed us one by one to jump into that choppy leviathan several feet below. There was no getting used to the water; it was either, "all in and swim" or "no go and ferry home." Most chose to go, but some chose no.

The moment came: the official pointed at me.

I mustered all my courage and leapt several feet off the ferry – my mind doing its best to prepare my body for the shock of the cold.

When I hit the churning water below I felt my goggles – so crucial to my ability to navigate – rip from my head. Knowing my swim was as good as over without them, I frantically searched for my goggles. On all sides people were jumping in, splashing water in my eyes as they hit, bumping into me as they began their swim.

In the midst of all the commotion, I managed to find my dislodged goggles and pull them back on. At first I was a little disoriented from the chaos of the jump and the goggles and the mass of other swimmers, but soon I found confidence in my preparation. I began to do what I had trained to do, swim to freedom.

Kick, stroke, navigate, breathe, move through the water and get to shore.

The swim was everything I expected and nothing I expected all at once. Yes, there were the tangibles, the cold water, fellow swimmers, and the current. All this I had anticipated intellectually. I knew quite well it was coming. But there was also the reality that I had never experienced anything like this before. I was, at the same time, completely ready and utterly unprepared for the swim ahead.

I had to rely on my focus on my goal of getting to shore. Kick, stroke, navigate, breathe, and move through the water – it was coming together. The familiarity was overriding the unknowns.

Until something I had not trained for happened.

4

From a few yards away, I heard a gurgled shout, "Help!"

At first I thought it was my own subconscious playing tricks on me, a shout from within, from a place that was still unsure of the swim ahead. But then I heard it again, louder this time: "HELP!"

As I stopped my stroke, another swimmer drafting behind collided into me. I could feel the current immediately pulling me away from my destination. I struggled with the fact that if I helped there was a good chance my race was over. Surely it was not my responsibility to help someone else. Heck, I was barely making it myself! Finally, squashing the selfishness inside, I swam over toward the call for help.

Scanning the water, I saw an arm flailing in the distance and swam toward it. By the time I reached the now almost catatonic swimmer, a fellow racer arrived on the scene. In unison we called for help, finally getting the attention of the patrol boat. Unfortunately, there were so many swimmers in the water that the driver couldn't navigate his boat safely over to us. A few long minutes later a kayaker with a water gurney came paddling up and was able to tend to the shell-shocked swimmer.

By this time the current had taken me quite some distance from the course, so with effort I struggled to reestablish my path, and began to once again attempt my swim to freedom.

Kick, stroke, navigate, breathe, move through the water and get to shore. The water was rough and the current relentless, but each cycle of my stroke moved me closer to my destination.

At times there was a swarm of swimmers all around me, and other times I felt that I was completely alone. For some reason it seemed easier when I was in a pack of other swimmers, but even that had its challenges. At about the halfway point, when I had finally settled in and was really finding my pace, I was suddenly pulled under water.

Completely submerged, and a bit panicked, thoughts of Jaws ran through my head. What had pulled me under? After a few frantic seconds I discovered the cause of my attack. Another swimmer had grabbed my foot and pulled me under. I am not sure why he did it; maybe he was panicked, maybe he was trying to sabotage my race. Whatever the reason it was so unexpected that it took me several seconds to get back into the rhythm of the race. But, again, my goal and my focus took over: kick, stroke, breathe, move through the water and get to shore.

After 54 minutes I finally reached the shore. A cheering crowd and, more importantly, my friends and family were there to support me in my "escape from Alcatraz."

A LIFE IMMERSED

Our faith journey is a lot like swimming from Alcatraz Island. We begin as prisoners to our brokenness faced with a choice. Are we going to serve a life sentence? Or are we going to try to make a break for it – and swim to freedom?

The leap from captivity to freedom can be daunting, even terrifying, as we move from the familiar (as bad as that might be) into the unknown. To be successful it is "all in and swim." There is no getting used to it, there is the ledge and there is the leap – and, waiting for us, the startling water of a complete immersion into faith.

Once we hit the water, unexpected things will happen to us. Perhaps our goggles will be knocked off by the sudden change in environment, as our world view is rocked by our encounter with the one and only living God.

While this is certainly a good thing, it can be scary nonetheless. The world we'd constructed suddenly taken apart and reordered is a frightening prospect, even when the reordering is an infinitely vast improvement. Often we also feel an overwhelming sense of hope flooding into our lives, a beautiful change, but sometimes hard to accept after years of skepticism and disappointment.

Along the way, once we think we are on track we press forward, struggling to stay on the right path, things may arise that make us question whether we truly are on the right track or not. So often these trials of doubt come from unexpected sources, like a fellow swimmer pulling us down as they struggle in their own swim to freedom. Or maybe we have to backtrack or seemingly veer off course to aid another swimmer who is in trouble. Will we find the course again? The doubts stack up quickly.

Through the hindrances and unexpected struggles, again and again we must regain our bearings and resume our swim to freedom. Breathing, navigating, kicking, and pulling for the goal, for ultimately a dry, secure shore awaits – and a host of those who cheer us on.

In the end, being fully immersed in the life God has envisioned for us depends upon the power of God who gives us the ability to finish the race. A life immersed requires that we first leap into the water, learn to breathe in the life giving spirit of God, use our minds to navigate toward the shore, use our strength to kick and pull our strokes, all in concert with each other. This is the redemptive struggle of our swim toward freedom in Christ.

SWIMMING THE GOOD RACE

"I have fought the good fight, I have finished the race, and I have remained faithful."

-Apostle Paul[1]

Jesus was tested by the religious leaders of his day in all kinds of subtle and not so subtle ways. One of these tests came in the form of a simple question. What is the most important commandment? In other words, what is the key to "swimming the good race" according to God? As usual, Jesus' response is both disarmingly simple and profound in its application:

---

[1] Tyndale House Publishers. (2004). *Holy Bible: New Living Translation.* (2nd ed.) (2 Ti 4:7). Wheaton, Ill.: Tyndale House Publishers.

The most important commandment is this: 'You must love the LORD your God with all your heart, all your soul, all your mind, and all your strength.' The second is equally important: 'Love your neighbor as yourself.' No other commandment is greater than these.[2]

Familiarity can be blinding. Psychologists Daniel Simons and Chris Chabris of Harvard University performed a fascinating study demonstrating that humans process very little information once we think we know the situation.[3] The phenomenon is called "change blindness," when a person only sees what he or she originally took in, blind to the true reality of the situation.[4]

Change blindness is the foundation of magic shows. The audience assumes the most obvious explanation: the hat is a regular hat; the rabbit is the same rabbit the magician just showed them, the pack of cards is a standard set of cards. This is all fine and dandy for magic shows, but when it comes to life, this blindness can have devastating results.

---

[2] Mark 12:29-31 (NLT)

[3] http://www.youtube.com/watch?v=mAnKvo-fPs0 Accessed 11/12/2010

[4] Daniel Simons and Chris Chabris, Gorillas in our midst: sustained inattentional blindness for dynamic events http://www.wjh.harvard.edu/~cfc/Simons1999.pdf Accessed 11/12/2010

The familiarity of "The Great Commandment" can be a stumbling block. It certainly was with me. The change blindness of what seemed to me like oversaturation in this verse left me thinking I understood it. At some point I stopped processing the depth and significance of Christ's answer to the Pharisees' question.

I have run into similar change blindness in others repeatedly over the past three years while working on my doctorate. When "churched" people asked me what my dissertation or book is about, I used to tell them: living out the Great Commandment in the 21st century. I found that as soon as I mentioned the Great Commandment their demeanor would change. It's become predictable, the sharp shift from interested to dismissive.[5]

Of course, the Great Commandment is not "old news." Christ is the very embodiment of the new. His command is the very core of what our lives are to be about. Jesus' answer to the question from the religious leaders states unequivocally what we are meant to focus on in life in order to achieve the prize. We are to holistically love God and love people.

This book is about answering the question, what would a life look like if a person loved God with all of

---

[5] It is telling that more than one church leader has come to me for insight into why their church is not making an impact in their community. Then they completely dismiss the Great Commandment as old news and complain that they had come to me for a *fresh* idea, a *new* program that would jump start their dying church.

the heart (emotions), soul (spirit), mind (intellect), strength (physical self), and loved others as themselves (social).

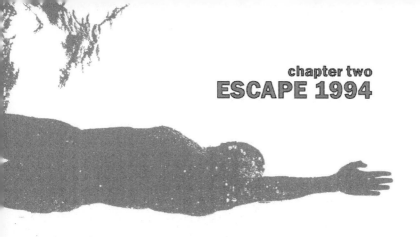

ESCAPE 1994

"I did it my way."
-Frank Sinatra

I did not follow Christ for most of my life. Up until June 1st 1994 I was more of a functional atheist than anything else. Until that day, I had been able to get by, to maintain a bearable level of worldly contentment and shallow distraction. I'd been able to effectively ignore the crucial shortcomings of my life.

But on June 1st 1994 all of that came crashing down. That was the day that my brokenness almost won.

I woke up that morning in Redondo Beach, California, in my dream home, with my dream wife of six months beside me in the bed, and my dream car in the garage. I was living the American dream.

I got out of bed with my standard ritual of stretches and groans, trying to exorcise the demons from the night before. Another night of giving in to my ignoble instincts. Another morning feeling older than I should.

As I walked into the bathroom to prepare for the day, I did something that I had not done for a long time. I looked directly into the mirror – and caught my own eyes looking back at me.

I quickly turned away, as if I had seen something I was not supposed to have seen. That response alone was condemning enough.

With great effort, I worked up the courage to look again. It was one of the hardest things I'd made myself do – every reflex in me resisting. I stared into the mirror, daring to look myself in the eye. I'd never truly understood the saying that the eyes are the window of the soul until that moment. As I peered deep into my broken and desperate soul I was frightened by what I saw…

...nothing.

I saw nothing! I looked and searched but all that looked back at me was a pair of empty eyes, drained of hope, passion, purpose, or reason to go on. I had so wrapped up my life in achieving goals to make me happy that when I had accomplished them I found I had nothing left. And worse, to my great despair, they had somehow failed to give me the fulfillment I was seeking.

That day I was faced with a sobering truth; I was spiritually, morally, and emotionally bankrupt. I had put all my hope that satisfaction and happiness would be achieved through a multi-million dollar home at the beach, a fuel injected V-8, and a wife that would cause my friends to writhe in jealousy.

All these great achievements and plans I had laid had not built what I thought they would. The truth was, all those years I had been subtly constructing my own prison, wall by wall, bar by bar. And now I was cornered, trapped, imprisoned – and, in a twist of tragic irony, I was both the builder and the warden.

All I could think of was that I needed to escape. And like all the needs of my life, I would have to meet it on my own power. I would free myself. It was decided. I would kill myself. If this were all there was in this world then I did not want to participate anymore.

I at least had enough respect for my new wife not to leave her to stumble over a corpse when she got home, so I decided that I would find my "freedom" outside the house. As I pulled out of the drive, I was trying to think of ways to make it look like an accident, so she could collect the insurance money and the family could avoid the shame.

At the time I worked in the heavy equipment rental business and a large part of my job was driving all around Southern California visiting different construction sites that needed heavy equipment to rent in order to do their work. I figured a tragic driving mishap might work. I could "lose control" and go crashing down the cliffs of Palos Verdes. This would accomplish both of my final goals – and add a dramatic finale to this whole fiasco.

Before I went for my final drive, however, I decided it would be helpful to all if I tie up some loose ends at work. I followed that familiar route and ducked into the office.

THE SMILE

While I was rummaging through some paperwork, something unexpected happened. My father walked in.

He was just dropping in to say goodbye before he went on a six month music tour.[6] A man by all accounts who had achieved respect and prestige on every stage he ever stepped onto. Artists from Jerry Garcia, John Denver, and Vince Gill all desired him to play his signature Dobro on their projects.

A casual visit with his son. I had not really talked with my father much in the months leading up to this day and his unexpected visit took me by surprise.

After some surface chatting about his upcoming tour, I decided to raise the stakes. I asked him if we could talk. He of course accepted the

[6] LeRoy Mack http://www.leroymack.com/

17

invitation, as that's always been his nature, but if he had any inkling about he was getting into, he didn't show it.

I took the chance and decided to open up to him, to be honest for the first time with another human being about how I was really feeling.

I told him about the emptiness I felt, how I hated the person I had become, how I had tried everything in this life to make me happy, and that I wanted to die. I didn't know how he would respond – if he'd be disappointed in my failure to create a meaningful life, or even dismiss this as overemotional ravings.

But he did neither. I'll never forget what happened next.

He smiled.

I had just told my dad that I wanted to die...and he smiled!

Right before I couldn't take it anymore, right before I ripped into him with some choice words of what he could do with his smile, he gave me the reason for the smile.

He said, "You haven't tried everything."

I assured him indignantly that I had. How could he know all the ways I'd tried to compensate for my increasingly hollow life? What had I not tried in all those years?

"No," he rebutted. "You have not tried Jesus."

This answer struck a bitter chord with me. With a touch of venom I replied, "Not this religion crap again."

"Not religion, son. A relationship with the one and true living God."

It was that day that I died to myself and became a new creation in Christ. The lifestyle changes soon after.

> **To watch a video about my journey with depression and anxiety please visit:**
> http://www.vimeo.com/14228663

THE CHANGE

My father encouraged me to go see a medical doctor and tell him about what I was feeling. So, my wife Shannon and I went to go see a mental health professional. With the three of us sitting together in his office he opened up a book and began to ask me a series of questions.[7]

"Do you have a lack of energy?"

---

[7] To see a list of depression and anxiety symptoms go to Appendix 5

"Do you have excess worry?"

"Are you irritable?"

Question after question I answered yes. After several minutes of this he finally closed his book and pronounced concisely that I suffered from depression and anxiety.

I insisted that this could not be. "I live at the beach, drive the car I want, have a boat and am married to a beautiful woman. I have nothing to be depressed about."

The doctor looked at me as if I were the biggest idiot in the world and gently said, "That might be, but nevertheless you are depressed and have anxiety."

Up until that point I had become a master of self-deception. I had bought into the worldview, which proclaimed that by having all your externals polished, life would be great. The only problem is by focusing all your energy on erecting a shiny façade it leaves your heart, soul, mind, and relationships empty.

Ctrl+Alt+Delete

"The LORD directs the steps of the godly.
He delights in every detail of their lives.
Though they stumble, they will never fall,
for the LORD holds them by the hand."
                                        -King David[8]

---

[8] Psalm 37:23–24 (NLT)

When your computer gets all buggered up and freezes on you, you don't throw it away (even though you may want to), you hit Ctrl+Alt+Delete to stop the function(s) that is making your operating system freak out. Our God not only allows for Ctrl+Alt+Delete in our lives, He is the author of it. When we overload our heart, soul, mind, bodies, and relationships and our lives freeze up on us and nothing is working as it should anymore, God is there, saying, "Hit Ctrl+Alt+Delete. Let's reset and go forward living life the way I created it to be lived."

On June 1st, 1994 I began a new life trusting that God would direct my steps. At times it was very difficult learning to trust Him. However, like any relationship, the more time I spent with Him the more I began to know His character.

What I have learned about God's character is that He is trustworthy. I can even trust that He allows my depression and anxiety to be in my life in order for His power to be shown through me. I can trust that an aspect of my masterful craftsmanship by the Master Craftsman is in fact this particular struggle.

That's easy to write, but it's hard to live. I've certainly had my times second-guessing God. In 2 Corinthians 12:8 Paul described his own similar struggle:

> Three different times I begged the Lord to
> take it (thorn in the flesh) away.[9]

I can tell you that I have asked God way more than three times to take away my depression and anxiety. Many of those times were not polite and I used language that would have caused my Mum to reach for the soap. I have explained to Him (convincingly, I thought) that if He took it away I could do so much more for Him. Sometimes I felt compelled to be a little more forceful in my rhetoric. All to no avail.

By evidence of me writing this book, God in His immeasurable mercy did not strike me down. Instead, He lovingly replied to my requests and demands with this profound and beautiful truth:

> My grace is all you need. My power works
> best in weakness.[10]

THE NECESSARY RESTART

A few years back, my wife Shannon told me something, well, shocking. She said my depression was the best thing that had ever happened to us.

To fully understand the counter-intuitiveness of this comment, you have to realize that this is the woman who I put through hell during some very rocky times at the beginning of this journey. Off and on for years I could not function; I was so debilitated by my

---

[9] 2 Corinthians 12:8 (NLT)

[10] 2 Corinthians 12:19 (NLT)

depression and anxiety that she often had to carry the emotional load of our marriage alone. Yet here she was telling me that it was the best thing that ever happened to us.

Her explanation surprised me. Before my depression I was arrogant, selfish and lacked empathy. But by being forced to hit reset I had become more humble, giving, and gentle with those around me. This desperately needed reboot cleared out a lot of the garbage that had built up in my life and allowed me to reset and trust God to be the leader of my life. God's hand in directing my life had profoundly changed me and in so doing saved our relationship. In essence, my insistence on controlling my life had prevented God's power to work in me.

In life you will make mistakes and there will be times that you will have to hit Ctrl+Alt+Delete again, but as you focus on what Jesus said are the most important things in life, loving God and loving people, you will move closer to the rich and satisfying life God envisioned for you. You must clarify in your heart and mind what is the best thing in life to focus on, not letting "good things" distract you from the best thing; the rich and satisfying life Jesus came to give you. The peace of mind to wake up each day knowing that you are on the right path to experiencing a holistically excellent life.

chapter three

Do you want to be healed?

> "When Jesus saw him lying there and knew
> that he had already been there a long time,
> he said to him, 'Do you want to be
> healed?'"[11]

When I first started training for competitive swimming, I struggled for about a year to get faster on my own. Finally, I came to the realization that my technique was more like prolonged drowning than the masterful swimming form of Michael Phelps. I needed help!

When I finally found an experienced swimmer willing to work with me, the first critical question he asked was, "Do you want to learn how to swim to win?"

I almost laughed at first at this question. Of course I did. Who wouldn't want to learn how to do something that would enable them to succeed? But then, I was told in order to swim to win, I needed to

---

[11] John 5:6 (ESV)

unlearn what I thought was competitive swimming and learn from scratch how to do it correctly. This prospect was not so obviously desirable.

He told me it was going to feel unnatural and wrong at first, but if I wanted to learn how to "swim to win" that I needed to trust him.

This was a big dilemma for me, I really didn't want to trash a whole year's work in the pool and start again from scratch. Couldn't I just tweak my swimming a little bit and be successful?

Ultimately, my desire to swim competitively outweighed my pride in my own efforts, and I finally submitted myself to the teaching of someone who had mastered the art of competitive swimming.

To begin our journey together, I need to ask you a question. A question that I want you to spend some time thinking about before you answer. A question that if answered honestly could change the rest of your life.

Do you really want to "win?"

To phrase it a different way, are you ready to discard the coping mechanisms you have developed to just get through life and start living out the rich and satisfying life God has envisioned for you? In other words, do you want to be *healed*?

This is not my question, this is actually a question Christ asked a man who had been sick for 38 years and had been reduced to a life of begging just to survive. It has always been fascinating to me. On one level it's almost, dare I say, absurd. If someone is sick or broken wouldn't they be desperate to be healed? Or to use the metaphor, if someone desires to be an effective swimmer, wouldn't he or she want to learn to swim to win? Why would Jesus ask this obvious question?

The question is especially curious when considering to whom he asked it. He was as low as you get, as desperate as you get, as sick as you get. And yet Jesus still asked the question, "Do you want to be healed?"[12]

Why wouldn't he want to be healed? Is Jesus being heavily sarcastic at a lowly man's expense? Surely not!

After a decade of being a pastor I believe God has given me some insight into why Jesus asked this question. In fact, I have found myself recently asking more and more people the same question.

This is the ugly truth about our brokenness; many of us do not want to be healed. It may be hard to believe that someone would not want to be delivered from their emotional, physical, or spiritual pain, but the reality is many of us do not. Many of us have become very comfortable with our brokenness and cling to it like a toxic friend; some of us have even found our identity in our emotional, physical or spiritual pain, and we simply would not know how to live without it if we were healed.

You see, unlike people, jobs, and churches, our brokenness will always be there for us. In fact, for many of us, it is the one thing in life that has always been there, and as bad as it may be, at least it is the devil we know.

---

[12] John 5:6 (RSV)

Jesus knew the compelling lure of security that captivity offers. The comfort of clinging to the railing of the ship, of knowing that tomorrow will be the same and that because of our broken condition, we will not be called upon to step out into the unknown. He knew that the fear of the unknown for the crippled man may be larger than his desire to be healed.

So he asked the obvious question, "Do you want to be healed?"

I often wonder what would have happened if the man had not gotten up. What if he just continued to sit there, afraid to leave the captivity of his brokenness? What if he had never plunged into the waters of the unknown and begun the swim for freedom? How long would Jesus have tried to convince him to pick up his mat before he moved on? A day, a week, a year? Would he have tried to convince him of his healing with empirical evidence? Or, would he have simply said, "Sit there if you want, but you are healed" and continued on his way..

So I ask again, Do you want to be healed? Do you want to accept the freedom that Christ offers? Will you pick up your mat and walk? Are you willing to find your identity in Jesus rather than your brokenness? Are you ready to plunge in, to be fully immersed? Or do you want to remain where you are, doing things your own way, dealing with the same issues?

If you honestly answered yes to Jesus the good news is that you can be healed. You can be healed from your depression, anxiety, obesity, anger, sexual brokenness, substance abuse, compulsive spending, and just about anything else.

How you may ask? The way to being healed is a complete surrender of your pride, your identity, and your life to Jesus. It is the commitment to holistically live out loving God with all your heart, soul, mind, strength, and loving others as yourself. Although this may seem overly simple, and maybe even simplistic, the reality is this: the path to true healing is a relentless pursuit of who God has envisioned you to be.

So, do you want to be healed?

chapter four

THE PERFECT PRISON

"We are all serving a life sentence in the dungeon of the self."

-Cyril Connolly

Sometimes we successfully escape from our cells only to find that we've brought the prison with us.

After God had freed me from my self-made prison, I soon found a new, far-reaching entanglement. A prison that followed me long after I left the shores of my personal Rock. The "perfect prison." Perfectionism.

Perfectionism, the belief that we must attain and maintain divine moral and spiritual standards, plagues the American church. Yet perfectionism in believers is the supreme tragic irony. Christ died to break our bondage from sin; but in the "Perfect" we find chains more subtle, and perhaps even more insidious.

The chains of perfectionism are long. They snatch at our ankles, so often dragging us under, long after we believe we're free.

GOD'S MASTERPIECE

"For we are God's masterpiece. He has created us anew in Christ Jesus, so we can do the good things he planned for us long ago."

-Apostle Paul[13]

There is a critical difference between being perfect and being a masterpiece. Being perfect is an unnatural state and for all rights and purposes useless in the real world. Being a masterpiece, however, is the result of our restoration by Christ to do the things God has planned for us long ago.

It's overwhelming. The Creator of the universe, the Creator of the moon and the stars, rainbow and the rose, the atom and the myriad galaxies, calls us His magnum opus, His masterpiece. Only the God of all creativity could conceive of such incalculable grace!

One of the defining characteristics of a masterpiece – regardless if it is a painting, sculpture, or poem – is its uniqueness, crafted by its creator. Masterpieces are things so unique that they transcend the world's primary motivation of greed and for this are considered "priceless." It's hard to imagine

---

[13] Ephesians 2:10 (NLT)

something so matchless and treasured that it cannot be purchased, but that is the very nature of a masterpiece.

Masterpieces are a gift to those who experience them. We are drawn to these inimitable and invaluable works of art because something about them changes us and enriches our lives. For this personal enrichment, people go through the enormous expense and hassle of travel just to be in the presence of the work. They have heard stories from others about their experience, how it changed their lives in some way, and they literally cross oceans to experience the same.

REPRODUCTION OR ORIGINAL?

The difference between a masterpiece and a reproduction is an immeasurable gulf. Even a skillfully and faithfully produced reproduction or copy of the original work of art holds nearly no value at all in relation to the original.

Take the *Mona Lisa* for example. If you were to visit the Musée du Louvre in Paris, France to experience this supreme example of Renaissance portraiture first hand, you would need to wait in line for hours and undergo extensive scrutiny from security personnel. After all this hassle you would be rewarded by being restricted to viewing the *Mona Lisa* in a climate-controlled room, for a few minutes, through murky safety glass. All that distance, all that time, for a glance through a dark glass.

Perhaps the most telling aspect of this pilgrimage to da Vinci is in the leaving. Upon exiting the Louvre, surrounding you on all sides are... hundreds of *Mona Lisas*. Being pushed for cheap purchase by hoards of street vendors, hundreds of exact Mona Lisa replicas go largely ignored by the exiting pubic. The original work, no matter its less than ideal presentation, is all that matters.

Masterpieces are original and – counter-intuitively for many of us – masterpieces are *not* perfect. In fact, in many ways, masterpieces are identified by their imperfections, their defects validating their authenticity.

Technology has grown to a point that we could take any of the world's priceless treasures and reproduce a replica that is without any of the "imperfections" left by the creator's hand. We could easily have a *Mona Lisa* with a less enigmatic smile, or a *David* with proportional arms.

In doing so, however, the work would not truly be improved; in fact, the masterpiece as it had been known would have been destroyed in the "perfecting."

In Ephesians 2:10 Paul states, "For we are God's masterpiece. He has created us anew in Christ Jesus, so we can do the good things he planned for us long ago."[14] We are a unique, priceless, creation crafted by the very hand of God and if we try to be someone else we vandalize the uniqueness that makes us God's masterpiece.

In my faith journey I had to embrace the truth that seemed so contrary to the view I held of myself

---

14 Ephesians 2:10 (NLT)

for most of my life. My past experiences, passions, and brokenness were not my unbearable burden, my permanent disfigurement. They were in fact the opposite. God's vast grace used them to mold and shape me into a priceless work of art.

This is your truth as well. You have not been called to be a replica of another masterpiece; you have been uniquely crafted by the Creator of the stars and the seas to reflect His plan and creativity.

IMPERFECT EXPERIENCES

"I will teach you wisdom's ways and lead you in straight paths."

-Solomon[15]

God has entrusted us with our past experiences to be a gift to those struggling to make it in this broken, messy world. These experiences do not disqualify us from ministry; they prepare us and give us credibility to those who are faced with the similar adversity.

I really struggled with this early on in my faith journey. My life before Christ had left a trail of broken relationships and an accumulation of scars from self-destructive behavior. I knew Jesus had forgiven me, but I was equally certain that my life choices had also disqualified me for any significant ministry. I was cornered by my own conflicting beliefs.

One day when I was particularly burdened by my perceived ministry disqualification, I stopped by a

---

[15] Proverbs 4:11 (NLT)

friend's office who was also the youth pastor at the local church I was attending. I unloaded on him, conveying my disappointment at being sidelined because of my past.

He paused for a moment then looked squarely in my eyes. The questions he asked were simple, but poignant:

"Have you ever killed someone?"

"No." I answered.

"Have you ever sold yourself for sex?"

I chuckled at the thought of it and answered,

"No."

"Have you ever committed adultery?"

Once more I replied, "No."

Then he leaned back into his chair and pronounced, "Yep, you are probably right. God can't use you."

At this point, I was confused. Was he saying if I am not a murderer, prostitute, or an adulterer that God cannot use me? He could see my consternation. He leaned forward into his chair and I could feel God preparing me to receive his words. What he said – so simply and matter of fact –was a truth that profoundly altered the rest of my life.

"Your past experiences do not disqualify you from ministry, they prepare you for ministry."

That moment marked one of the great turning points of my faith journey.

My friend's statement is not some postmodern pithy truism; it comes straight off the pages of the Bible. All one needs to do is open up the Bible to Hebrews 11, often called the "Faith Hall of Fame," and see who is listed. The writer of Hebrews points out undeniably that the world's worst are often God's best.

Noah was a drunk.
Abraham slept with his maid.
Sarah laughed at God.
Jacob was a deceiver.
Rahab was a prostitute.
Moses was a murderer.
Gideon was a afraid.
Barak was a coward.
Samson was promiscuous.
David was an adulterer and a murderer.[16]

And the writer of Hebrews doesn't even get into the lives of the New Testament murderers, persecutors, prostitutes, and divorcees.

I don't think any of these guys would be on the modern American church's shortlist for potential

---

[16]Hebrews 11: 7, 8, 11, 21, 23, 31, & 32.

ministry leadership. Clearly, God's criteria are vastly different than our own.

You see, God has entrusted us with our past experiences in order to prepare us to be the tangible hand of Christ. This is a truth that the enemy desperately wants to keep from us, because those who have heard and believed this truth have become very dangerous for the cause of Christ.

THE GIFT OF PASSIONS

"Do we all have the gift of healing? Do we all have the ability to speak in unknown languages? Do we all have the ability to interpret unknown languages? Of course not!"

-Apostle Paul[17]

I remember a group of guys who liked to hang out and work on their cars. It was something they were passionate about; they'd get together and help one another and chat about the latest breakthroughs in oil or coolant (or whatever it is car people talk about).

One day I was talking with one of them because he did not feel that he had anything to offer God in service. He told me that he was not a musician or a preacher; he also said he could not see himself doing children's ministry (nor could I) or any other churchy type job.

---

[17] 1 Corinthians 12:30 (NLT)

Then I asked him, "What do you love to do?"

"You know, work on cars."

"Right, why not use the passion God has entrusted you with?"
"How so?"

"Why don't you and your friends one Saturday a month offer to do oil changes and other car maintenance stuff on single mothers' cars?"

"Would that count?"

I assured him that it would "count" and I had no doubt that it would be an amazing blessing to the single mothers in our community.

I have had a version of this conversation hundreds of times with different people who have hundreds of different passions. I've heard about passions for things mundane and obscure. Passions for sewing, baking, party planning, painting, and gardening; and passions for back-up singing, screenwriting, and triathlons (of course I had to throw that one in there). God's creativity in instilling diverse passions in his people has continually amazed me every time the issue arises.

Sometimes it just takes a little mind time to see how our passions can be used for God's glory, and shared in community as a way of loving others.

THE GIFT OF BROKENNESS

"To keep me from becoming proud, I was given a thorn in my flesh, a messenger from Satan to torment me and keep me from becoming proud. Three different times I begged the Lord to take it away. Each time he said, "My grace is all you need. My power works best in weakness." So now I am glad to boast about my weaknesses, so that the power of Christ can work through me."

-Apostle Paul[18]

Not only has God entrusted you with passion, God has also entrusted you with something most people believe to be a hindrance. Brokenness. Like passion, brokenness is meant to be a gift to others.

But how can this be? Isn't brokenness usually a cause of separation between people? An alcoholic's binge drinking certainly is no "gift" to his loved ones!

True. But that is brokenness *mishandled*, brokenness that is not brought to the foot of the cross.

The bond of brokenness is powerful. While it can be abused – allowed to be waved about like a white flag of surrender, or conspicuously worn like a badge of honor – if it is truly given over to God, the perfection of his imperfect creations becomes clear. We are able to love other imperfect beings because of our own imperfection. The bond between those

---

[18] 2 Corinthians 12:7-9

who share a similar "thorn in the flesh" can be powerful in a loving community.

The bond of brokenness is not its only gift; it is also an undeniable call to humility. God has built in us a governor, a limit to our abilities, a constant reminder of our need for Him.

I love how Paul does not reveal the details of the "thorn in the flesh" that was afflicting him. In this way I think he is able to convey a concept with which we all can identify: brokenness and pain in our life that God will not take away for some reason.

I have heard people identify their "thorn in the flesh" as sexual brokenness, substance abuse, and selfishness. For me, my thorn in the flesh is depression and anxiety.

Brokenness is a strange force in this life. It can be the thing that destroys us, defines us, or the very thing that God's power works through to make us a blessing to the world we live in. In 1991 my brokenness had nearly destroyed me and my family. But in God's economy of grace, that brokenness was turned to blessing.

chapter five

New Definition of Winning

"If you ain't first, you're last."
-Ricky Bobby, *Talladega Nights*

THE LIFE GOD ENVISIONED

Jesus tells us that he came to give us "a rich and satisfying life."[19] Surely this is good news! "Rich and satisfying," or in some translations "life abundantly," who doesn't like the sound of abundance, richness, satisfaction?

But what does Christ really mean by a "rich and satisfying life"?

Is it a vacation home in the Hamptons, a primary residence in Beverly Hills, and driving a Lamborghini? Most of us have had enough life experience to at least be deeply suspicious of such a shallow definition of "rich and satisfying." Certainly there's enough contrary evidence in the tabloids to encourage us to search in a less materialistic direction.

---

[19] John 10:10b (NLT)

So is it living a "good" life? Investing time in our families, being honest and upright, building a good reputation. That's certainly not falling for the materialistic trap. Surely investing in our families is more along the lines of what Christ was talking about. Honesty, integrity, good repute – these are certainly biblical principles. Something straight out of Proverbs can't steer us wrong?

But then... the inevitable failure. I find myself unable to invest the time really needed for my wife and kids. I find my white lies morphing into something darker. I find my reputation is less than squeaky clean. In short, I find myself falling short of the good life.

So maybe richness and satisfaction comes from somewhere else. Perhaps it depends on someone else, someone other than me.

Most of us have tried and failed to experience a "rich and satisfying life" under our own power; many have even given up on pursuing it anymore. Trying to construct a rich and satisfying life based on our own personal accomplishments will only lead to disappointment. The Apostle Paul talks about how everyone has gotten off course in life and because of this Jesus came to show us the way.[20] His way requires full immersion. It is holistic, involving every aspect of ourselves; and it begins and ends with dependence on Him.

THE WAY

Maybe the way to experiencing the rich and satisfying life Jesus spoke about – the very same rich and

---

[20] Romans 3:23 NLT (insertions mine)

satisfying life which has eluded the human race since its inception – is a complex simplicity which has been hidden in plain sight for thousands of years.

Maybe it is all about focusing on the right thing. Winning!

A NEW DEFINITION OF WINNING

Most Christians do not like to talk about winning. They feel it somehow makes them sound arrogant or unspiritual, but the Apostle Paul speaks about winning. Most famously he said it this way (for the purpose of this book I changed Paul's metaphor of running to swimming):

> *Swim* to win! All athletes are disciplined in their training. They do it to win a prize that will fade away, but we do it for an eternal prize. So I *swim* with purpose through the *water with every breath, navigation, kick, and stroke.* I discipline my body like an athlete, training it to do what it should. Otherwise, I fear that after preaching to others I myself might be disqualified.[21]

There are lots of good things you can do in this life. In fact you can spend your whole life doing *good* things and miss the *best* thing – what God has envisioned for your life. To be fully immersed in the life God has envisioned for you requires you to swim "to win," that

---

[21] 1 Corinthians 9:25-27 (NLT, insertions mine)

you do so with "purpose" all the while "practicing discipline like an athlete."

This famous passage from Paul's letter begs the question: What is *winning*? In the metaphor, it's reaching the shore and finishing the race. In one sense, then, we might define winning as reaching heaven, arriving at the ultimate shore, the divine finish line of the race of life.

But is that true? Is Paul only talking about eternal life? Can we "win" in this life, in the here and now?

DQed

Paul is certainly talking about heaven on one level, but he also speaks openly about his fear of eventually being disqualified from completing the race. There is nothing worse than training for a race, then competing in a race, then at the end finding out that you have been DQed (disqualified).

My ten year old son Eric is an avid triathlete. He trains hard and he wants to win. Last year it was his goal to qualify for the IronKids National Championships. This required him to finish in the top five of his age group in a qualifying race; no easy task.

Eric focused a great deal of energy on one particular IronKids qualifying race. I remember watching my son come flying out of the water, his pace perfect for his target time. He had a flawless transition and was off on the bike course, looking stronger than ever. All his training was paying off.

After he transitioned to the final leg of the tri, the run, we figured he was in a great position to achieve his goal. Eric would finally make it to Nationals.

We watched with great anticipation, counting athletes in his age group, waiting for him to round the corner. We cheered as he rounded the corner, right on his qualifying pace, and shifted into his final sprint.

Waiting for the results seemed to take forever. With hundreds of other parents and athletes we eagerly watched the head ref begin methodically posting the official results.

We gradually pushed our way to the boards and began scanning the pages. Where is he? We know he finished, so why wasn't he listed with his fellow athletes?

Finally, with trepidation I scanned the DQ listings. And there he was, Eric McNees.

Apparently there was some confusion on the bike course (possibly a timing chip failure) and he got DQed. The dejection washed over my son immediately and powerfully. All that training and the false sense of triumph in a hard fought race. It was crushing, especially for a ten year old.

I am happy to say that Eric learned an important lesson that day about knowing the course and he did qualify for Nationals at the next race.

From my readings of Paul's letters, he seems as concerned with how you race, as he is with the other side of life's finish line. Running the race without being DQed requires knowing the course God has laid out for you to run and to run that course as an ambassador of Him. As you race toward the finish line, you are to run in a way that brings God's Kingdom here on earth as well as in Heaven.

WINNING *IN* THE RACE

Winning is experiencing what God originally envisioned for his creation. In other words, winning is becoming fully human, becoming what God created us to be. That might make some sense from a theological or semantic perspective, but what does that mean for us practically?

We were created to have an intimate relationship with our Creator. There have only been three people ever to walk this planet who have experienced being fully human; Adam, Eve, and Jesus. Being fully human is having an unbuffered connection and interaction with God.

Since the Garden, however, we've lived buffered lives, a disconnect present because we have elevated our own vision for our lives over God's vision for our lives.

Our relationship with God is like any relationship in our life. It is a constant battle with our selfish nature, the battle between our own selfish desires and the desires of the person with whom we are in a relationship. Our relationship with God is damaged when we choose our own selfish desires over God's desire to be intimate with us. This results in a rift with our true soul mate, leaving us feeling the profound dissatisfaction of a buffered life.

Paul describes this buffered state as feeling as if we are looking "through a glass, darkly"[22] – experiencing life as if looking through a clouded window, ever separated from the true life that awaits us on the other side. However, we don't have to resign ourselves to a clouded and shadowy existence. We are not hopelessly condemned to a buffered life.

The essence of the Gospel is that God loved us so much that he sent his only Son to pay the price for our rebellion. He came to remove the buffer, break down the barrier between us and Him. To restore our full humanity.

This sacrifice and redemption is free – in fact, it is freedom itself. That is, it does not have a price we must meet nor is it forced upon is. Jesus did not come as a stalker to force us back into a relationship with God; he came to give us the opportunity to move toward the relationship we were designed to experience. For those of us who choose to move into this relationship, we have the hope, that someday we will experience what it means to be fully human.

For now, we are like the Apostle Paul who said, "No, dear brothers and sisters, I have not achieved it, but I focus on this one thing: Forgetting the past and looking forward to what lies ahead, I press on to reach the end of the race and receive the heavenly prize for which God, through Christ Jesus, is calling us."[23]

---

[22] 1 Corinthians 13: 12 (KJV)

[23] Philippians 3:13-14 (NLT)

What is the heavenly prize? Being free to be "fully human," to experience an unbuffered, unfettered intimacy with God.

YADA YADA

*"Seek his will in all you do, and he
Will direct your paths."*
-Solomon[24]

The word from Solomon's proverb that the NLT translates "seek" is *"yada"* in ancient Hebrew. *Yada* is an extremely powerful word meaning, "to know by experience."

One day while I was letting this word, *yada* marinate in my brain I remembered an old episode of Seinfeld where Jerry was dating this girl who would complete her sentences by saying "...yada yada." She would say things like, "I went out to a club last night and *yada yada*, and I'm really tired this morning."

This became the whole premise of that particular Seinfeld episode, Jerry, George, and Elaine using the phrase, "yada yada" to create an open interpretation of an event.[25] This particular episode

---

[24] Proverbs 3:6, (NLT)

[25] "The Yada Yada" is the 153rd episode of the American NBC sitcom Seinfeld. The 19th episode of the 8th season, it aired on April 24, 1997.

was especially popular; in fact, it was nominated for an Emmy. But why was this so funny?

My theory is the audience would know *by experience* how to fill in the *yada*. What Jerry's girlfriend means by *yada* is something like, "you know the rest of the story by experience." The connection for the audience was the experiences of their lives – some similar or even shared experiences, some singular and unique. But the personal and madlib-esque possibilities of how to fill in the *yada yada* is the heart of the humor.

TO KNOW BY EXPERIENCE

Solomon is a master wordsmith, choosing his words with great deliberation. Consider Proverbs 3:6 if we translate it with this more precise definition of *yada*:

> *"Know by experience his will in all you do, and he will direct your paths."*

This closer reading potentially changes the meaning of this scripture from an intellectual pursuit of God's vision for our lives into a full immersion into the experience of a life of faith in Christ.

There is a profound gap between intellectually *knowing* the Great Commandment and knowing the Great Commandment *by experience*. To know God and live out the vision He has for our lives we need to go beyond an intellectual knowledge that we are to holistically love God and love people; we are to know this *by experiencing* it.

All people go through adversity. You have gone through it, you are going through it, or you are going to go through it. When you are in the darkest times in your life do you want your faith based on an intellectual knowledge of what someone told you? Do you want to rely on something you read in a book? Or, do you want to move forward because of *yada*, you know by experience that God is faithful and will make your paths straight?

I have had the privilege of standing with people through their darkest times. There is a big difference between people who have *yada* faith and people who have an intellectual faith.

In a tragic turn of events, a man in my church lost his eye sight, a devastating occurrence that broke my heart for him and his family. The greatest testimony of his faith was that he knew that God would make it work together for good. To my knowledge he never had self-pity or got angry, he just kept moving toward Jesus.

How can this be? It is because he *knew by experience* that God would make it work together for good.

Through his continued spiritual insight in the state of physical darkness he has become an inspiration to all who know him. He has amazed us with the books he has continued to write and vision he continues to share.

God intends for His sons and daughters that they know Him by experience. To know the story of God because you experienced it. That is our pursuit. That is our ultimate passion, to *yada yada* with God.

Instead of standing on the ferry, pondering the water, you need to jump in and swim, to experience the life God has given you, to tirelessly pursue His vision for your life. This requires full immersion, all of you, a holistic experiencing of life. It requires giving your heart, spirit, mind, and strength to God. It requires giving over our relationships, trusting them to Him. It requires a holistically excellent life.

A HOLISTICALLY EXCELLENT LIFE

"Since you excel in so many ways—in your faith, your gifted speakers, your knowledge, your enthusiasm, and your love from us—I want you to excel also in this gracious act of giving."
-Apostle Paul[26]

In his letter to the believers in Corinth, Paul commends them about excelling in so many ways; living a life of excellence. How their faith, speaking, knowledge, enthusiasm and love was excellent and an inspiration to others. But, what *is* excellence?

First, let's start with what excellence is not:

     1. Excellence is not perfection.
     2. Excellence is not common.
     3. Excellence is not expected.

---

[26] *2 Corinthians 8:7–15 (NLT)*

Imperfect

Excellence is not perfection. Perfectionism is a destructive trap that leaves its victims hollow and depressed. Perfectionism also steals the joy of grace that Jesus offers His creation. When perfectionism takes root then nothing is ever good enough and nothing is ever complete. Perfectionism at its worst can stop someone from living out the vision God has for their life because they never think their gift is good enough to share. I have seen this happen too many times. A person that God has wonderfully made and designed to be a gift to the world never offers their gift because they fear their gift is not perfect. When this happens the enemy wins. You are not perfect, but you can be excellent.

Uncommon

Excellence is not common. Excellence is not perfect, but it is not common either. The definition of excellence is, "an outstanding feature; something in which something or someone excels."[27] Common is, well, common. It is all around us and there is nothing special or extraordinary about it. God has not called you to live a common life; He has created you to live an extraordinary life, a life marked by excellence; anything less is sin.

Unexpected

Excellence in not expected. In life we have been conditioned to expect mediocrity. We expect service

---

[27] Compliments of thefreedictionary.com.

at a restaurant to be mediocre, we expect movies to be average, we expect our churches to be boring. We do not expect excellence because it would only lead to constant frustration. Every so often though we are surprised by excellent service, an exceptional movie, or a challenging and engaging worship gathering and we are energized by the experience.

So, what *is* excellence?

Excellence is a gift!

THE GIFT

A gift is anything that is beyond what is common or expected. If you buy a double-half-decaf-giraffe coffee from your local coffee house and you pay your money and you get your drink, that is not excellent or a gift. But, if you go to your local coffee house and order your double-half-decaf-giraffe coffee, and you are greeted with a warm, genuine smile and an authentic (although short) conversation from the register host, and when the barista hands you your drink you notice that in the foam they have drawn a little giraffe, you have now experienced excellence.

Why? Because although none of these things were perfect (smile, conversation, drawing) they were uncommon and unexpected. These things were a gift from them to you, to make your day a little better. That is excellent.

At the end of each of the five main chapters of this book we will have a short discussion about what it means to be excellent – relationally, spiritually, intellectually, physically, and socially. We will also discuss several tangible expressions of how to live out this holistically excellent life.

Living out the life God has envisioned for you, a rich and satisfying life, means not just finishing the race in the future sometime, but racing with purpose, integrity, and strength. Racing in a way that when you do cross the finish line God will say, "Well done my good and faithful servant." The race is hard at times and we will be tempted to take shortcuts along the way or just give up, but God is with you every step of the way. His power is perfected in your weakness and the great thing is he wants you to know Him and know by experience that He is there for you. Ultimately, He has created you in this place and this time to be an unexpected and uncommon gift to those around you.

"Excellence is a gift; be generous."

Group Swim
the great commandment

Group Swim
Section 1
Jump In:

(You can't swim unless you are in the water. The "Jump In" is an "ice breaker" question to get the group talking.)

What is the biggest adventure you have ever been on?

Drill Set:

(Drills in swimming are used to improve speed and efficiency. Studying scripture in the same way refines the heart, soul, and mind to help us live out the vision God has for our life.)

Read: Mark 12:28-31

What would someone's life look like if they lived out The Great Commandment?

Read: John 10:10 & John 17:13

Why did Jesus say he came in John 10:10 & John 17:13?

What does Jesus mean by a "rich and satisfying" life?

The word "rich and satisfying" in the Greek is "perissos" meaning: advantaged or exceptional.

Do you think there is a connection between what Jesus said is the most important thing to do in life (Mark 12:28-31) and a rich, satisfying, and joyous life (John 10:10 & John 17:13)?

Do you think if someone lived out The Great Commandment that they would live a richer and more satisfying life? Why or why not?

Do you think most Christians are experiencing a rich and satisfying (exceptional) life?

Read: Matthew 28:18-20

Rhetorical question: Do you think most people are attracted to the exceptional or the ordinary?

If Christians are not experiencing an exceptional life, what impact would it have on fulfilling Jesus' instruction to make disciples of all nations?

What is the relationship between The Great Commandment (Mark 12:28-31), a rich and satisfying life (John 10:10), and The Great Commission (Matthew 18:18-20)?

Open Water Swim:

(An open water swim is the real deal, no walls to hold onto, plastic lane lines to keep people from bumping into you, or black lines painted on the bottom to keep you going in the right direction. This section is a suggestion for the participants in your group to go out and put into practice the scripture that was studied.)

Over the next 40-days commit to discovering what it means to live out loving God with all your heart, soul, mind, strength, and loving others as yourself.

Jesus' final instruction to His follower was:

- Make Disciples
- Baptize them
- Teach them His commands

Matthew 28:19–20 Therefore, go and make disciples of all the nations, baptizing them in the name of the Father and the Son and the Holy Spirit. Teach these new disciples to obey all the commands I have given you.

The only command Jesus gave his followers was:

- Holistically love God (Heart, Soul, Mind, and Strength)
- Love others as ourselves

Mark 12:30–31 ...you must love the LORD your God with all your heart, all your soul, all your mind, and all your strength.' The second is equally important: 'Love your neighbor as yourself.' No other commandment is greater than these."

By living out the Great Commandment we will live the life God has envisioned for us:

- Rich
- Satisfying
- Joyous life

John 10:10b My purpose is to give them a rich and satisfying life. **& John 17:13b** I told them many things while I was with them in this world so they would be filled with my joy.

When you put the Great Commission, Great Commandment, & RSJ you get a picture of a fully devoted follower of Christ life.

part 2
Water
loving God with all your heart

chapter six

TIDES OF TROUBLE

"Most of us are swimming against the tides of trouble the world knows nothing about, we need only a bit of praise or encouragement – and we will make the goal."

Jerome P. Fleishman

When people find out that I swam Alcatraz, they usually ask me, "How far is it from the island to shore?" I tell them it is one and a half miles, if you could swim straight to shore. Only problem is you can't.

San Francisco Bay can have currents of over six miles per hour. Even a well-trained competitive distance swimmer can only swim around 2.5 miles per hour. Clearly, without some planning, the tidal current is going to win every time.[28]

---

[28] NOAA Tides and Currents for San Francisco Bay, http://wolfweb.unr.edu/homepage/edc/tides/2010/sfgg_fr 10.html (accessed 9/22/2010).

A quick glance at the NOAA Tides and Current chart for San Francisco Bay is enough to see there's an ebb and flow to the bay tides, swinging sometimes by as much as eight miles per hour.

To compensate for this wildly variable current, master swimmers have calculated the optimum time to swim from the island to the shores of San Francisco.

When I swam the Bay, the organizers had us hit the water when the current was between two and three miles per hour. In the pre-race meeting we were instructed to swim 90 degrees out of line of where we actually wanted to end up.

Intellectually, I got the science of it easily enough. It made perfect sense: if I wanted to swim from Alcatraz Island and end up just past Marina Green, I needed to swim 90 degrees askew from my ultimate destination – and the three mile per hour current would land me right on the beach. So, what's the issue?

I found out during the swim that what I knew in my head and what I felt in the water were two vastly different things. What was the disconnect?

First, you cannot feel the current when you are in it. I kept on second guessing what I was told about the speed of the current because I simply could not feel it. I kept thinking to myself that they must have made a mistake. All of my instincts overrode the master's instructions; certainly I could just swim toward the beach....

Second, swimming 90 degrees in the wrong direction of your destination, when wind waves are knocking you around, never feels like the best plan. In my swim to freedom I had to decide if I was going to trust my instincts and feelings, or the instruction of a master swimmer who had made over 100 successful swims from Alcatraz Island to the shores of San Francisco.

SUBMERGED COPING MECHANISMS

Often in the difficult hours of life I find I am guided not so much by wisdom and biblical principle than by instincts and feelings. Reflexes and emotions arise naturally, seemingly to guide and can even feel as if they are a great protector, but navigating life this way has the potential to lead you astray.

But when the moment has passed and I have re-gathered my senses and remembered my spiritual instruction, I find that these feelings and instincts are not the saviors they seem. They are not inborn saving graces – they are submerged coping mechanisms. And, inevitably, they end up proving to be more destructive than productive forces in my life.

I am often in conversations with people who argue over the practicality of biblical principles. It's the "real life doesn't work that way" conversation. One of a pastor's top five most frequent dialogs.

My typical response runs something like this (though perhaps with a little more grace): "If your 'real life' way has worked so well, then why are you in the mess you are in?" If following "real life's" instruction techniques – instincts and feelings and worldly logic – works so well, why are we having the conversation to begin with?

Loving God with all one's heart is patterning one's emotional life to glorify Him. To do this one must trust Him – emotionally resting in the certainty that He has the best vision for our lives, even when it goes against initial instincts.

Many times following God's path feels like swimming at a 90 degree angle out of line from our destination. But we are told in 1 Corinthians 1:27 that, "God chose things the world considers foolish in order to shame those who think they are wise."[29]

Paul is warning followers of Christ that when they live in accordance with scripture it may seem foolish to some who think they have a monopoly on practical knowledge, but ultimately God will prove that His wisdom is higher than the wisdom of man.

THINGS I WISH WERE NOT IN THE BIBLE

I often joke with people about doing a series at our church called, "Things I wish were not in The Bible."[30] In this series I would go through the things in The Bible that go against my instincts. I would include things like, giving the first portion of your income to God, keeping the Sabbath[31], and loving others as yourself.

These biblical instructions do not make emotional sense; they fly in the face of my innate selfishness. Just try to rationalize how giving away 10%

---

[29] 1 Corinthians 1:27 (NLT)

[30] Element3 Church www.element3.org

[31] Sabbath is giving a day to focus having a right relationship with God and people.

of your income as a good financial move, or, how much sense does it make that spending a day away from work will help advance your career, and how can putting others needs on the same level as your own be a positive in your life?

These scriptural ideas are counterintuitive, 90° – if not 180° – out of line with how most of the world conducts life. But we are reminded by God that, "For just as the heavens are higher than the earth, so my ways are higher than your ways and my thoughts higher than your thoughts."[32]

THE CURRENT IS STRONGER THAN YOU THINK

I think most of us underestimate the power of our emotional current.

The authors Chip and Dan Heath address this concept in their book, *Switch: How to Change Things When Change Is Hard*. They point out that the powerful influence of the emotions on human psychology has long been understood. To prove their point, they paraphrase Plato's *Republic*: "in our heads we have a rational charioteer who has to rein in an unruly horse that 'barely yields to horsewhip and goad combined.'"[33]

They go on to reiterate an analogy about the tension between our mind and our emotions that was

---

[32] Isaiah 55:9 (NLT)

[33] Heath, Chip and Dan Heath. *Switch: How to Change Things When Change is Hard*. NY: Broadway Books, 2010. Page 6.

used by University of Virginia psychologist Jonathan Haidt in his book, *The Happiness Hypothesis*:

> Our emotional side is an Elephant and our rational side is its Rider. Perched atop the Elephant, the Rider holds the reins and seems to be the leader. But the Rider's control is precarious because the Rider is so small relative to the Elephant. Anytime the six-ton Elephant and the Rider disagree about which direction to go, the Rider is going to lose. He's completely overmatched.[34]

There are tools and methods we can use to help control our elephant, but we need to realize that sometimes we are at the mercy of our emotional pachyderm and we need to have given people the relational right to help us during those times.

SWEPT AWAY

When I was nine years old, I visited some family friends in Portland, Oregon for a week of hiking, fishing, and adventure. During one particular excursion along the river, we were having a ball picking blackberries, skipping rocks, and splashing around. Along the way, the dad of the family I was staying with told us that we need to cross the river in order to get to our destination.

---

[34] P. 102-13.

As I looked across the rapids I knew that there was no way I would survive trying to cross the rushing white water. I made a covenant with myself that no matter what, I would never go anywhere near this part of the river.

"Not here," said the dad, seeing my anxiety rising. "We will cross up the river a little ways where the current is not as strong."

That was a relief to my young ears. So up the river, we went. After a mile or so, with an abrupt stop, he declared, "We'll cross here!"

Now, in my nine-year-old mind, this crossing was still scary, but after some encouragement (i.e., being told I had no choice), I started following the dad across the river. He told me to follow in his footsteps and everything would be fine.

Step after step I moved deeper into the river, with great care I tried to follow the dad as closely as possible. The rocks underneath my feet were smooth and slippery, and with each subsequent step the pressure of the current increased against my weakening legs.

Suddenly, without warning my feet came out from under me and I found myself being dragged down the river. One moment I was in control and, the next, at the complete mercy of the rushing river.

With all my might I struggled against the current, trying to get back to shore – to safety – but no matter how hard I tried to fight, the river was stronger.

My arms flailing to keep my head above water, I now was entering the part of the river where I swore I would never go, the rapids. With a burst of adrenalin I frantically tried to get to safety, knowing that once I entered the white water all would be lost.

My body was thrown around like a rag doll, hitting bolder after bolder as I gasped for breath between desperate moments underwater. Although I could see people on the shore trying to help there was nothing they could do. I was on my own.

Upon entering the first part of the rapids, I was introduced to a bone crunching bolder. After smashing me into it, the current lifted me up and over the rock, finally plunging me into the depths below.

When the terminal hole[35] finally released me back into the rapids, I managed to get my head above water once again. Down the river I saw a man on the other side standing on a fallen tree.

"Swim over here!" he shouted, waving his hands.

My mind rushed with thoughts of survival. He was farther away than the shore I had been struggling to reach. But, I'd had no luck trying it the other way. With some misgivings, I decided that I would try to make it to him.

As I got closer I noticed that the current was not as violent and the rocks seemed to be below me instead of in my path. While I was making progress, I

---

[35] A terminal hole is a hole in a river bed that usually follows a rapid. If a person is ejected from the raft and falls into a terminal hole they will be sucked in and the water rushing over the top will hold the person under.

could tell that I was not going to make it to him in time.

Continuing to struggle to get to him, I saw someone running toward the man with a large branch. About the time I was going to pass them by, they both had reached the end of the fallen tree – and held out the large branch. I maintained hold long enough for another man to jump off the fallen tree into the water, grabbing me and the limb just as my hands gave way.

WHO TO TRUST?

"Then Christ will make his home in your hearts as you trust in him. Your roots will grow down into God's love and keep you strong."

-Apostle Paul

The difference between my successful crossing of the San Francisco Bay and my near death experience in the river came down to who I trusted and their assessment of my capacity to make the crossing. The master swimmers had successfully made the swim hundreds of times in many different conditions, they knew the tides and currents; they also knew our abilities as swimmers based on our previous races. The dad although well intended, had never crossed the river before and had no idea if a nine year old boy could make it or not; he just *felt* it would be ok.

All of us have a limit on our emotional capacity. Some of us can withstand strong emotional currents, ones that would sweep away another person; the experiences, psychological makeup and maturity level allows the emotionally strong to conquer greater currents. It is important to know and respect your emotional capacity in order to live out the life God has envisioned for you. We are all different; some of us thrive and are energized by contact with people, while others of us are drained by social interaction. It is imperative for you to know what situations lift you up and which ones push you into an emotional tail spin. It is also crucial for you to know which people give you energy and which people in your life drain your energy. But most of all it is vital to have people (or a person) in your life who you trust more than your out of control elephant.

I have a few people in my life that I trust more than my feelings. These are people who are fully devoted followers of Christ who will speak God's truth into my life which is based in scripture. I will not seek advice from people who may be well-meaning, but are not living a life which I wish to emulate.

Think about it this way. You would not get financial advice from a friend who is broke, or relational guidance from someone who has left a trail of broken relationships. In the same way you should not trust your heart to anyone except those who desire to have Jesus make your heart His home. When the peace of Christ is at the center of your emotional life, His love will strengthen you to have faith that will transcend your circumstance. The Apostle Paul, experienced this strength when he wrote, "I know how to live on almost nothing or with everything. I have learned the secret of living in every situation, whether it is with a full stomach or empty, with plenty or little. For I can do everything through Christ, who gives me strength."[36]

---

[36] Philippians 4:12–13 (NLT)

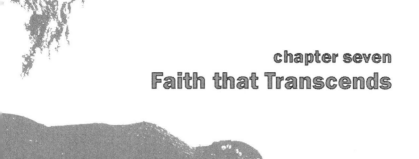

chapter seven

Faith that Transcends

"So Peter went over the side of the boat and walked on the water toward Jesus. But when he saw the strong wind and the waves, he was terrified and began to sink. "Save me, Lord!" he shouted."[37]

Water is unpredictable. One moment it may be a calm paradise and the next a turbulent hell. Emotions are a lot like water; our circumstances can change in an instant, a troubling phone call in the middle of the night, finding a winning lottery ticket, a drunk driver running a red light, or your spouse surprising you with a thoughtful gift. Circumstances, both good and bad can greatly affect our emotional wellness and the condition of our heart. That is why we need to anchor our heart in the bedrock of God's love which will withstand the tides of trouble.

---

[37] Matthew 14:29–30

Several years ago I was given a frightening and life changing lesson about the power and volatility of water and the importance of fixing my eyes on Jesus in the midst of the trouble. These were things I thought I knew about. But one terrible Saturday I quickly learned otherwise.

THE FISHING TRIP

This particular Saturday began like most others. I woke up to the alarm clock buzzing at 3:00am and the smell of freshly brewing coffee. I quickly slapped the alarm, jumped out of bed, grabbed my coffee, and headed down to the marina for another exhilarating day of fishing the local islands.

When I arrived at my boat, I took a minute to appreciate the sleeping marina and the glassy ocean water before disrupting the serenity by firing up the boats engines. By the time my fishing friends showed up, the sun was imbuing the sky with brilliant red rays and the seagulls had begun their daily ritual of picking through society's refuse for their breakfast. Yes, it was going to be another perfect day.

There is nothing like quietly cutting though the calm water while exiting your home marina. It had become like an old book I've read a hundred times before: familiar, predictable, a classic. On my port side we passed the harbor patrol, while the sea lions were busy trying to steal fish from the bait barge on my starboard. After passing the fishing pier and rounding the breakwater, we always ceremoniously took off our hats in respect for the lighthouse right before we throttled down and planed out for the next couple of hours on our way to Santa Barbara Island.

The day was beautiful and clear, the fishing was great, it was everything I loved about the ocean and fishing. But like all things, that too must end, and it was time to head home. Our normal procedure was to listen to the weather before heading back. But the day had been so calm and the wind had never even picked up, so a weather check never really crossed our minds as we left the protection of the island.

About ten miles into our return trip the wind kicked up at 25 knots with a wind wave of 2 feet. This was not unusual, except for the fact it was coming from the southwest, not the northeast. A slight cause for concern, but nothing a 28' sport-fisher with two engines couldn't handle. And, besides, there was only 30 miles left till the entrance to our marina.

MAYDAY

Five rough miles later, things had become significantly worse; the wind was now blowing consistently at 40 knots with 5' wind waves. The biggest problem was that now 12' ocean swells had picked up from the north leaving us right in the middle of an ancient struggle between wind and water – a struggle where thousands of seamen before us had paid the price of ocean passage with their lives.

Suddenly, a strong 60 knots gust grabbed our boat and tore the Bimini top off the fly bridge, dragging it into a collapsing swell. Water was crashing in on us and with a huge roar one of the engines stopped running. We knew we were in trouble, but did not know the extent until I went into the engine compartment. With waves and wind crashing around me, my heart sank when I saw the reality of the situation: We were going to die.

The force of the last wave was so great that it tore the exhaust manifold from the hull of the ship. We were taking on water, fast! I am not sure what you would do at this point, but one of my friends took off his pants and threw them at me. Normally I would not be too receptive if a man took off his pants and threw them at me, but in this case it was an act that would save us from sinking down into Davey Jones locker.

I took the pants, diverting my violated eyes from my rather large, hairy, pantless friend (who thankfully was not going commando that day). I shoved them into the hole with a feeble hope of slowing the water coming into the boat. Amazingly, it slowed the water down enough that our bilge pump could keep up with the water intake and slow our sinking.

Now, with only one engine and the weather getting worse I worked my way to the radio and spoke a word three times that I prayed would never come from my lips; Mayday, Mayday, Mayday....

FROM TERRIBLE TO TERMINAL

After telling vessel assist our position and our situation they informed me that the weather was too bad for them to come out. They would need to send the Coast Guard. As soon as he spoke those words we were hit by a 10' wind wave, which hurled us into the now giant swells coming from the north. Our 10,000 pound, 28' boat was picked up like a toy, spun around and slammed back into the water.

Picking up my aching body from the latest wave, I realized that things had just gone from terrible to terminal. There was no electrical or mechanical power on the boat and the only noise I heard was that of the roaring winds. By this time my two friends had given up hope and went below deck to await the inevitable.

I was our only chance for survival. A survival that looked impossible, considering we had no engines and no electricity to power the radio to call for help.

I knew that I needed to get the bilge pump going because without it we would sink in about thirty minutes. So I lifted up the engine compartment's overhead doors, chained them open, and climbed into the darkness with a little flashlight. I stepped into two feet deep water and started getting shocked by the eight batteries that had been ripped out of their holders and now laid spread all around the half-submerged engine room.

Thrown around by the waves and burned by the electricity, I somehow managed to pull a battery out of the water, connect the bilge to it, and get it pumping. This was only a momentary triumph though, because another big wave hit our now seemingly tiny boat, breaking the engine compartment door chain and sending it crashing down on my head. As I slipped into unconsciousness my last thought was how

I needed to stay awake because otherwise we were going to die.

THE UNANSWERED CALL

I don't know if it was one minute or one hour later but I woke up lying in the bilge being shocked by the electrified water. In a daze I remember I had a handheld radio for emergencies down in the cabin. I made my way down into the cabin in the dark, found the radio and began my distress call again.

"Mayday, mayday, mayday..." but this time there was no response.

Climbing back out on deck with the hope of better reception I tried it again: "Mayday, May-Day, MAY-Day..." And, again, no response.

The little hope I had to this point turned to anger. I had done everything I was meant to do – I had even bought a backup communication device and it was not working. Despite my despair – and since it was all I had – I kept on calling with no response. In-between my unanswered calls, I kept bailing water with an old pot I had, just trying to keep us alive a little longer.

LIGHT ON THE HORIZON

At about 2am my anger turned once again to hope when I saw a light on the horizon. Could this be our salvation? Could this be someone to help us? I tried the radio again to no avail and decided to fire off some flares. My hope faded as I watched our savior's light move into the darkness. In desperation I called on the radio again and again, "Mayday, May-Day, MAY-DAY..."

Though there was no response, I did see the light reappear in the distance. It seemed to be heading in our direction, so I called again, "MAYDAY, MAYDAY, MAYDAY..." No response, but the ship was definitely coming closer.

With renewed hope, but still the need to keep afloat, I got back in the bilge and bailed. After getting the water level down again, I popped back up to see where my rescuer was. To my dismay it was going about 45 degrees in the wrong direction.

I tried the radio again, "MAYDAY, MAYDAY, MAYDAY..." there still was no response; but, the ship did seem to change course and head back toward us. Finally, through crashing waves and unbelievable gusts of wind the huge white ship with the letters U.S.C.G came into clear sight and saved us from marinating in the Pacific.

After a long night of being towed back to the marina we arrived safely into the harbor at about 10am. During the post rescue interview I asked the Coast Guard Captain how he found us. He told me that even though we could not hear them, they could hear us, and every time I called them they were able to get our coordinates, enabling them to come and save us.

MAYDAY OF THE HEART

Our emotions, like water can be turbulent and have us calling out to God, "MAYDAY, MAYDAY, MAYDAY! God I'm drowning down here!" We want God to save us right now, we want an answer, but many times because of our circumstance we cannot hear Him.

But there is the good news! He hears us and He is with us, even if we cannot hear or feel Him during our storm. In Isaiah we are told "Don't be afraid, for I am with you. Don't be discouraged, for I am your God. I will strengthen you and help you."[38]

It is important to know that God is bigger than any storm you will ever face. The wind may blow and the waves may rise, but if we keep our eyes fixed on Jesus, He will see us through the storm. You may feel alone and that no one is with you, but God is with you, the hand of Christ is always on you no matter how overwhelming the tempest rocking your life.

---

[38] Isaiah 41:10 (NLT)

chapter eight

THE HAND OF CHRIST

Sometime when I am sitting with my wife reading, she will put her hand on my leg and just leave it there. At first it brings comfort and reassurance, but after a while it gets a little hot and uncomfortable. Eventually, even though her hand is still there, I don't notice it anymore; it is almost as her hand has become part of me.

The strangest part of this cycle is when she moves her hand to do something else, it is like losing an integral connection that I did not even realize was still present.

I believe many of us have experienced the same phenomenon with Christ's hand. For those of us who have walked with Him for many years, we remember that initial comfort and reassurance we felt when He first laid his hand on us. The peace and calm. The certainty of God's love and direction. The freshness of the newfound relationship with our creator. We glory in His hand guiding us.

However, after a season of His guiding hand leading us into this new life, we start to get a little uncomfortable. We may even think about removing His guiding hand. For those of us who resist the temptation to reassert control over our lives, we get to move into an integrated relationship with our Creator, where our connection becomes part of our very existence.

At times this can be scary because we have become so familiar with His hand that we do not even feel it anymore. But have confidence: He is with you.

In Psalm 16:8, David wrote, "I know the Lord is always with me. I will not be shaken, for he is right beside me."[39] The Lord is also always right beside you as well.

ENTER THE DRAGON

One of my favorite movies growing up was Bruce Lee's 1973 classic, *Enter the Dragon*. In the film Bruce Lee's character is recruited by a government agency to infiltrate the compound of a drug lord. Lee is invited to a tournament being held on the drug lord's island.

A crisis point in the film is the crime lord's realization of Lee's plans. Suddenly what was merely a game becomes a very real struggle for freedom and life.

In a similar way, the following will take a real life, practical turn, where I will provide some ideas that have helped me pursue living out The Great Commandment. Similar practically applicable subchapters will be included in the major sections of this book.

---

[39] Psalm 16:8 (NLT)

EMOTIONAL COMMUNITY

One of the most counterintuitive aspects about experiencing an emotionally healthy and balanced life is the fact that self-focused healing only makes you worse off. Several years ago, I was reading about a presentation given by a renowned psychiatrist about mental health.[40] During the question-and-answer period of his talk he was asked, "What advice would you give someone who is suffering from depression?" His answer surprised his audience, and quite frankly me as well. He said, "I would tell them to lock up their home, go across the railroad tracks and serve someone in need."

A broken heart and emotional brokenness thrive in isolation. The psychiatrist wasn't saying that medical attention for depression has no value; he was saying that we greatly underestimate the power of how serving others contribute to mental health.

THE MAGNET AND THE ANCHOR

I keep a dry erase marker in my car, so when an idea comes to mind I can write it on my windshield to keep it in front of me.

The other day while taking my son to school, he asked me, "Why do you have a magnet and an anchor drawn on your windshield?" I told him that it is to remind me that there are two people in this world, magnets and anchors. Magnets pull you up and

---

[40] Psychiatrist can prescribe medication a Psychologist cannot.

anchors drag you down; it is vital to know who is who in your life.

When I am having anxiety about a situation I will go to the magnets in my life and ask them if what I am feeling is reality. They know that I am relying on them to subdue the raging elephant and guide me through the water. This is not easy, but sometimes the current is too strong for us to navigate it alone.

It is essential to know which people pull you up to living out God's vision for your life and those who pull you down. As best you can you need to adjust your pattern of life to maximize encounters with the magnets and minimize your encounters with the anchors. By doing this you will experience a more emotionally healthy and balanced life.

"THERE IS A WAY."

Attitude is better than a crystal ball when it comes to predicting the future. If you have a poor attitude things are always going to turn out, well, poorly. If you have a positive attitude, things more often than not are going to end up being a positive in your life. The common saying, "perception is reality," is true; it's all how you view a situation or problem that determines how you approach it.

My dad, when I was growing up, had cards printed that read, "There is a way." He would hand them out to his customers and others to remind them that all problems could be solved. He even went so far as to strike the word, "problem" from his vocabulary, he would simply substitute the word, "opportunity" and operate from that perspective. I believe he, consequently, experienced a richer and more satisfying life because of his positive perspective.

DIVE INTO THE S.E.A.

When I am emotionally down I have an acronym representing three steps that help me feel better: S.E.A. This acronym stands for Sun, Exercise, and Authenticity.

The first piece of advice might make some overzealous dermatologists flush with irritation. Get some **sun**. Sounds simple, right? Well, it is – and it isn't. The fact is that sun raises you serotonin levels, which is the chemical in your brain that is God's given antidepressant.[41] When I am down, even 10 minutes in direct sunlight can lift my spirits.

You may not feel like **exercising**, but numerous studies have shown that just 30-minutes a day of exercise can raise your serotonin levels.[42] I have found that a walk, jog, or swim (any cardio exercise) will lift my spirits quicker than anything else.

Be **authentic** with a close friend who will love on you. Oxytocin is another hormone that can raise your spirits; sometime this hormone is called the "cuddle hormone." Oxytocin is released into our bodies when we feel loved and comfortable. There are some

---

[41] http://www.webmd.com/mental-health/news/20021205/unraveling-suns-role-in-depression

[42] http://www.livestrong.com/article/22590-effects-exercise-serotonin-levels/

studies that suggest that it can even be more helpful in fighting depression than serotonin. So, if you are hurting emotionally, be honest with a friend and let them love on you a little bit.

DO I HAVE THE RELATIONAL RIGHT?

Have you ever wondered why you can receive criticism well from one person and not so well from another? It may not be the criticism that is the problem; it may be the person giving it.

All too often people are readily willing to point out where you failed without any interest in walking the path that will bring success. Criticism without emotional investment in seeing the person live out their best is not helpful; quite the contrary, it can be very damaging.

In a practical sense, I ask myself a few questions before pointing out a perceived shortcoming of another person.

1. **Do I have the relational right to speak into this person's life?** To have a relational right to speak into someone's life you must have first spent time with that person, encouraged him or her, established a commitment to that person that extends past the current situation.

2. **Will I walk with this person to help them live out the vision God has for their life?** A real relationship is not telling someone that they missed the mark, now go fix it. Relational Right comes from sitting down with

83

someone and saying, "Hey, I believe God wants more for you than you are currently experiencing and I want to help you experience the rich and abundant life God wants for you."

3. **Is the problem the problem?** Many times the evident symptom is not the cause. Be cautious not to be so overly zealous to fix a symptom that you miss the bigger issue in someone's life.

Healthy relationship are not absent of conflict, in fact the hallmark of a healthy relationship may very well be the presence of tough conversations. In Proverbs 27:6 we are told, "Wounds from a sincere friend are better than many kisses from an enemy." If growth was easy they would not call it "growing pains" and those pains sometime come from a sincere friend who has earned the relational right to tell us the truth. Just make sure you don't get bit from behind.

EMOTIONAL EXCELLENCE

"So whether you eat or drink, or whatever you do, do it all for the glory of God."
-Apostle Paul[43]

.

---

[43] 1 Corinthians 10:31 (NLT)

Pursuing emotional excellence depends upon protecting and growing your relationships over the span of your life. The depth of connection and longevity of the relationships you share with people in your life I refer to in shorthand as the "relational quotient" (RQ).

A person who has a low RQ will leave a stream of short and broken relationships in their wake. Conversely, a person who has a high RQ will experience long and meaningful relationships. In order to pursue a higher RQ you need to be a gift giver. The gift? You. Your time, your energy, your attention. You.

The quality of your relationships will ultimately determine the quality of your life experience. You can have money, power and influence, but if you do not have anyone to share your life with, at the end of the day you will be unfulfilled (trust me on this). Money, power, and influence are poor substitutes for authentic, caring relationships.

The secret that Jesus hid in plain sight is the path to a rich and satisfying life is having a right relationship with God and people, and realizing that the rest is just commentary. At the end of your earthly life, the only things that matter are the relationships you invested in and the life tapestry you wove with those around you.

The ultimate beauty and value of this relational tapestry is determined by the threads that are woven in and by the threads that are torn out. A large relational tapestry that is woven over a lifetime with diverse colors and textures will produce a depth that is unique and priceless. Subsequently, a diminished relational tapestry that has been tattered and torn by the removal of threads will be regarded with little more value than a rag.

Relationships are hard, but we know that things of value do not come easily; relationships take a lifetime of work. Money, power, and influence may be what the world tells us are the keys to happiness, but if you want to be truly rich in this life, then invest your time and energy in weaving a large, colorful, unique, relational tapestry.

Again, emotional excellence does not mean perfection in all your interactions, but it does mean that you desire to be uncommon and unexpected in your relationships.

What is a common and expected friend?
- Someone who knows you on sight.
- Someone who will Facebook you on your birthday.
- Someone who knows enough about you to engage in a surface level conversation.

What is an excellent friend?
- Someone who thinks about and looks out for their friend's best interests; even when they are not around.
- Someone who will sacrifice their time for their friend.
- Someone who will speak truth into their friend's life in a loving way.

Emotional excellence is hard; it requires us to be gift givers. It requires us to go beyond the common and expected and to be extraordinary in our interactions with one another.

"Excellence is a gift; be generous."

Group Swim

water

Group Swim
Section 2
Heart

Jump In:

(You can't swim unless you are in the water. The "Jump In" is an "ice breaker" question to get the group talking.)

Who was your first best friend?

How did you meet?

What did you like to do together?

Drill Set:

(Drills in swimming are used to improve speed and efficiency. Studying scripture in the same way refines the heart, soul, and mind to help us live out the vision God has for our life.)

Read: Deuteronomy 4:29

Who are we promised to find if we search for him with all our heart and soul?

Read: Deuteronomy 11:16

What can happen when our heart is deceived?

Has your heart ever been deceived? What happened?

Read: Joshua 24:23

What "idols" do you have in your life that you need to destroy?

Read: 1 Kings 11:1-11

What was Solomon's sin?

What was the consequence of his sin?

How was Solomon's heart turned from the LORD?

What can this tell us about how the enemy steals our heart for our true love?

Read: Ecclesiastes 3:11

What has God planted in your heart?

What is our heart's limitation?

Is this limitation encouraging or discouraging to you?

Open Water Swim:

(An open water swim is the real deal, no walls to hold onto, plastic lane lines to keep people from bumping into you, or black lines painted on the bottom to keep you going in the right direction. This section is a suggestion for the participants in your group to go out and put into practice the scripture that was studied.)

Jesus said, "Don't let your hearts be troubled. Trust in God, and trust also in me." (John 14:1) Even though our hearts have eternity planted in them we cannot see God's whole plan. Trust that he will make all things work together for good if you love him. (Romans 8:28)

part 3
Breathe
loving God with all your soul

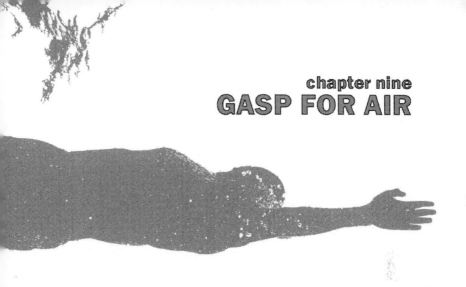

chapter nine
GASP FOR AIR

"It's not coincidental that psychology is the study of the soul. Psych comes from the Greek word for soul, breath, life. It is specifically the study of human conditions outside the physical domain. Is it possible that much of what we call psychosis and neurosis is really about us being soul sick?"

-Erwin McManus[44]

A SUFFOCATED SPIRIT

Swimming assumes moving forward. If you are not moving forward, you are merely floating, adrift in the current. Whether in the San Francisco Bay or in life, the reality is the same. It is either a deliberate swim or a passive resigning to the whims of the water.

---

[44] McManus, Erwin. Soul Cravings: An Exploration of the Human Spirit. Thomas Nelson Inc. Nashville, TN. (Page 10).

When you are living without intentionally, not moving toward the life God has envisioned for you, you are living a life without purpose. The truth about the "unintentional" life is it denies you the fullness of what it means to really live.

In Romans 6:23 (MSG) Paul writes, "Work hard for sin your whole life and your pension is death. But God's gift is *real life*, eternal life, delivered by Jesus, our Master."[45]

In other words Paul is saying that you can devote your life to things other than God's vision for your life and your reward will be spiritual death, but you don't need to suffer that fate because God has created you for a purpose.

There are many reasons why people don't or feel they can't move toward the goal of the life God has envisioned for them. Some start the race but physically wear out. Others falter mentally, for lack of preparation or planning or understanding. Others experience a failure of the will, losing interest in working so hard and just giving up. Sometimes others impede the person's progress, other swimmers pulling them under.

All of these factors – physical exhaustion, emotional depletion, intellectual stagnation, or relational pain – can impede your progress, but there is one factor when absent that can stop you dead in

---

[45] Peterson, E. H. (2002). *The Message : The Bible in contemporary language* (Ro 6:23). Colorado Springs, Colo.: NavPress.

your tracks to living out the vision God has for your life and that one factor is a suffocated spirit.

"YOU ARE THE AIR I BREATHE...."

> *"Then the LORD God formed the man from the dust of the ground. He breathed the breath of life into the man's nostrils, and the man became a living person."*[46]

The breath of God gives life to our form. Without it we are nothing more than a physical form, void of life. The Spirit of God is referred to as "Pneuma" in the Greek or "Air." For most of us *air* is not something that takes up a lot of mind time; unless of course, it is not there.

I mentioned that while I was swimming from Alcatraz there was a stretch where I had settled into my pace and felt I was really making progress toward the shore. Kick, stroke, navigate, breathe, and move through the water. Everything was going just as planned, until suddenly my forward progress was stopped – and I was pulled under the water.

At first I did not know what happened, was it a shark or a person? Why would a person pull me under? If it was a shark, why did I still have a foot? All great questions that ripped through my mind, until one thought became dominant.

---

[46] Genesis 2:7 (NLT)

"I need to get to the surface so I can breathe!" Suddenly, all other possible issues evaporated. Nothing was more important than air.

Isn't that true in life? We don't think about the really important things, unless of course they are not there. Relationships. Food. Water. Air.

I often hear struggling Christians holding up the Garden of Eden or paradise as the ideal state of a life without need. The reality is though that paradise was not a place without need; in fact, the Garden was a place full of need.

God created us to be constantly in need. We need to have caring relationships. We need nutritious food, we need clean water, and we need air. The hallmark of *loving God with all your soul* is not demonstrated by the lack of need in your life, but your acceptance that God is the fulfillment of your need.

From the moment God breathed life into Adam, he was in need of another breath. There were also four rivers that ran through Eden to quench his need for water. God provided animals and fruit trees to fulfill his nutritional needs. He created Eve to provide for Adam's companionship needs. And, above all, God was there to realize Adam's need for unconditional love.

YHVH

Rabbi Lawrence Kushner talks about how the very name of God is a reminder of our reliance on Him. He says,

The letters of the Name of God in Hebrew are YOD, HAY, VAV, and HAY. They are frequently mispronounced as "Yahveh." But in truth they are unutterable. Not because of the holiness they evoke, but because they are all vowels and you cannot pronounce all the vowels at once without risking respiratory injury.

This word is the sound of breathing. The holiest Name in the world, the Name of the Creator, is the sound of your own breathing.

That these letters are unpronounceable is no accident. Just as it is no accident that they are also the root letters of the Hebrew verb "to be." Scholars have suggested that a reasonable translation of the four-letter Name of God might be The One Who Brings Into Being All That Is. So God's Name is the Name of Existence itself. And, since God is holy, then so is all creation.[47]

Is it true that every time we breathe we are saying the name of God? We can't know for sure, but if it is, what a powerful reminder of our reliance on Him. Just imagine, every time we breathe we are

---

[47] http://rabbipaul.blogspot.com/2010/01/breathing-name-of-god.html

proclaiming that He is the source of our life by saying His name.

THE CONSTANT SOURCE

I think we often forget about the life giving power of God's constant presence. One night, soon after my acceptance of Christ, while lying in bed with my wife who was fast asleep, I began doubting God's presence and power in my life. I remember lying there saying to God, "if you are there I sure don't feel you."

After tossing and turning, it was as if God spoke deep in my soul, as if to say, "You are not sure if I am with you? Let me hold my breath for a second, just to show you how much I am with you." At that moment, my body went cold and I broke out into an icy sweat.

Shannon woke up instantly and said, "What's wrong!" I told her that I was doubting God's presence in my life and He showed me that He was here. "Well, don't do that!" she said – and went back to sleep.

God breathed life into us and we have needed Him for every breath since that day. The good news is that He is a constant source of pure oxygen waiting for us to breathe Him into our soul.

THE REJECTED/ACCEPTED WEDDING GUEST

"Can we boast, then, that we have done anything to be accepted by God? No, because our acquittal is not based on obeying the law."

-Apostle Paul[48]

---

[48] Romans 3:27-28 (NLT)

Many of us struggle to accept this breath of life and the reality of His love for us. It is hard for us to imagine that the creator of the universe who knit us together in our mother's womb and knows every hair on our head would sustain us so persistently, so unconditionally. Surely, we think, we must *earn* his sustenance.

While I was at a Growth Group (what we call our small group Bible studies), my Mum, who was visiting my family in Florida, recounted a story from my wedding to the group.

I had forgotten about it, but as she told it the memories of a dear friend came flooding back.

As I've mentioned, I was a rebellious and a self-destructive person before I surrendered my life to Christ. That being the case, I had collected quite a gallery of beautiful disasters as friends along the way. Naturally, many of these friends were either invited to the wedding or part of the wedding party.

At the time, my wife was a Banquet Captain at the Torrance Marriott; because of her job, we were able to get a great deal on having our wedding there. As most wedding days go, it was hectic and stressful, what felt like an overwhelming amount of activity whirling around us.

Unknown to me – while I was busy in the groom's room, tightening my tie and fixing my cuff links – one of my beautiful disasters had shown up to the hotel. He was dressed in an old t-shirt and ripped up jeans. While he was trying to enter the lobby, he was stopped by security because of his disorderly appearance and was being abruptly escorted out.

Luckily, the commotion caught my Mum's attention. She immediately went and got me to let me know what was happening.

I rushed out to the lobby to see my friend arguing with security outside. I quickly went out to them and put my arm around my rather, uh, informally attired buddy and assured security that he was not just a friend but an invited guest.

Life and our life choices take their toll on us, and so often in the view of others or even ourselves it may not seem that we belong. But God so loved us that he came to our rescue.[49] He met, and continues to meet, our need. He created our need for Him – and that need is good.

We are in need of rescue, beautiful disasters stumbling into the wedding. Our spirits are not independent, healthy bridesmaids and groomsmen, they are desperate for His life-giving Spirit, for Him to gently lead us into his celebration.

SUFFERING THE GIFT

Accepting God's breath of grace and forgiveness is hard to do. Our guilt instincts rail against the gift; we feel that we must somehow pay for our wrong doing, that we must earn God's gift of life.

---

[49] John 3:16-17 "For God loved the world so much that he gave his one and only Son, so that everyone who believes in him will not perish but have eternal life. 17 God sent his Son into the world not to judge the world, but to save the world through him."

One time while I was in Guatemala, we were invited to an open house celebration of a home our church helped build for a single mother. When we arrived the whole village was there to greet us and excited to show us the meal they had prepared for us to eat.

While we were walking over, a local pastor friend of mine whispered in my ear that the meal we were about to eat was their most special national dish and that the whole village had to sacrifice greatly in order to prepare it for us.

I've got to tell you that I felt a great burden of guilt about these extremely impoverished people sacrificing for me. I told my pastor friend that I did not feel that I could accept this gift, with all this poverty and hunger around me. He stopped and looked me straight in the eye and said, "Do not dishonor their sacrifice."

This is what another one of my friends calls "suffering the gift." You suffer the gift, when you know you have received something at the sacrifice of another. Suffering the gift is what many of us do with God's sacrifice of His Son, but it is that gift that brings our spirit to life. His grace is the air we are gasping for.

chapter ten

TRAIN YOUR EAR

"Why isn't that bush burning up?
I must go see it."
-Moses[50]

One question I am often asked is, "Why can't I hear God anymore?" Can it be that God has stopped speaking to us? He's finally gotten fed up with speaking to largely unresponsive sons and daughters, and is letting us endure an awkward silence or two. Maybe God's just feeling antisocial...?

The truth is God never withdraws His presence and guidance from our lives. His Spirit is always talking to our spirits. If there is a season of apparent silence, it is inevitably that we have tuned Him out.

I used to lead musical worship every Sunday in the church youth group I served in for many years. During that time in my life I played the guitar every

---

[50] Tyndale House Publishers. (2004). *Holy Bible : New Living Translation.* (2nd ed.) (Ex 3:3). Wheaton, Ill.: Tyndale House Publishers.

day and I became very good at discerning whether or not my guitar was in tune.

Yet this was not always the case. When I first began playing guitar I needed the assistance of an electronic tuner. After spending many hours with my guitar in my hands I eventually could tell if my "E" string (or any other string) was too flat or too sharp. Eventually I was able to get it back into tune without the assistance of an external device.

I could do this because of all the time I spent with my guitar, listening to it. I knew what an "E" string sounded like and when it was not right, I knew it. The only time that I needed the help of a tuner anymore was when there was too much external noise for me to hear my guitar well.

I haven't played my guitar with any consistency for years. I have been busy with other stuff and I just don't play nearly as much as I used to. The other day my son (who is taking guitar lessons) wanted me to play with him. I took out my guitar and tried to tune it. It was frustrating. Though I knew it was out of tune, I could not for the life of me get it dialed in. In frustration, I finally got out my electronic tuner to make sure I got it right.

I think training our ear to God's voice is a lot like training our ear to music. The more time we spend with Him the more we know his voice, His Spirit, and when He is speaking.

I love the description of Moses' encounter with God in the burning bush, "Why isn't that bush burning up? I must go see it."

Notice his question. He first had to recognize something was unusual. He could have very easily kept doing what he was doing, attending his flocks. But he was *aware* that something was unusual and tuned his attention and followed his curiosity to something outside his original plan for the day. It was not until Moses deviated from his plan and followed his curiosity that he heard God's voice.

The story of Moses records the first steps of the refining of an ear for God. Moses realized that every bush is burning and that every burning bush is an encounter with God.

The question is not, is God speaking to you? The question is, Will you be aware of the burning bushes around you? Will you tune your ear to hear Him and follow your curiosity away from your predetermined path you have previously chosen?

How you answer will impact your ability to hear what God is saying. Like Moses we have life to attend to and tasks to perform: the frightening thing is how often we struggle to hear God over the noise of our to-do lists. Sometimes it's a matter of moving out of the noise pollution, setting our plans aside for a moment, in order to see that every bush is burning.

How to Train Your Ear

Training your ear to God's voice and subsequently breathing in God's life giving Spirit comes down to immersing yourself in His presence. In my life, I have found that reading scripture, praying, musical worship, giving, and serving are the breath of God.

Read Scripture

> *All Scripture is God-breathed and is useful for teaching, rebuking, correcting and training in righteousness, so that the man of God may be thoroughly equipped for every good work.*
>
> *-Apostle Paul[51]*

The Bible is full of narrative, poetry, and teaching that was given to us to train our ear to the heart and mind of God. While scripture does not speak explicitly about every situation you will face in your life, it does give you the foundational principles to equip you to live out the life God has envisioned for you.

If you are not reading your Bible you are depriving your soul of air, a kind of self-induced asthma.

Growing up in Los Angeles in the 70s, at the height of the smog epidemic, there was many a day that we could not play outside because of a "smog alert." A "smog alert" was issued when some government official thought the percentage of air pollution might prove damaging to young lungs (or so they said; my theory was that they were intentionally trying to deprive us of recess). So when an alert was delivered, the (unfortunate for us) dutiful teachers would make us play Eye Spy, or something else likewise intolerable, in our classroom.

---

[51] 2 Timothy 3:16–17 (NIV84)

Most of the "smog alerts" were in the summer, however, when we were out of school. Most parents in the 70s weren't hypersensitive about their kid's safety like they are now. Parents today (myself included), baby our kids and would surround them in bubble wrap to keep them safe if we could. It is no wonder our nation has a childhood obesity problem considering the sunscreen, helmet, knee pad ritual we make our kids go through if they want to go play outside. Heck, if I had to go through all that, I would probably just stay inside and play Halo as well.

So, given the different parenting practices then compared with now, our parents would just ignore the silly "smog alerts" and let us swim and play outside all afternoon long. It was not until the evening that we would feel the effects of that lovely LA air in our not-so-pink lungs. I remember many an evening lying on the floor gasping for air, lungs hurting, and promising myself that I would not repeat the same mistake again the next day (which I always did).

Smog is not smoke+fog as they tried to make us believe. Smog is a lot of carbon dioxide in the air. Humans can't breathe carbon dioxide. There is no substitute for clean air – trust me on this. More importantly, there is no substitute for the Bible when it comes to giving your spirit a breath of fresh air. As Paul says in 1 Timothy 3:16, "All Scripture is God-breathed." In other words, scripture is the very breath of God, invigorating us, purifying our lungs, healing our spirit.

Prayer

> Don't worry about anything; instead, pray about everything. Tell God what you need, and thank him for all he has done.
>
> -Apostle Paul[52]

I get it. Prayer for many people is the last thing they utter after they misjudged a blind corner on a mountain road and they are plummeting to their death. Or, at best it may be something they do at their grandparents' house before dinner.

To many people, talking to God seems weird and maybe even a little crazy. For others even if they did want to pray they wouldn't even know where to begin. It really isn't as strange as you might think, if you don't talk to God now start small; tell God one thing you need and thank Him for one good thing in your life.

See, it wasn't that hard.

Ultimately, you want to get to a point where you "pray without ceasing,"[53] but "do not babble repetitiously like the pagans, for they think that because of their many words they will be heard."[54]

How do you pray without ceasing, but not babble?

---

[52] Philippians 4:6 (NLT)

[53] 1 Thessalonians 5:17 (ESV)

[54] Matthew 6:7 (LEB)

In a conversation with a friend, you would not just keep repeating the same phrase to them again and again; that is what little kids do and it is annoying. What grownups do is have thoughtful exchanges with each other, where one person listens and the other one speaks. Again, God is the author of relationships and the same rules that apply to your earthly relationships apply to your relationship with God.

Musical Worship

Psalm 95:1 Come, let us sing to the Lord! Let us shout joyfully to the Rock of our salvation.

Singing and music has a way of bringing happiness into a person's life. Who hasn't had the experience of being in a bad mood only to have a favorite song comes on the radio and before you know it you're singing and smiling like a fool.

When you combine singing and music which is directed toward exalting God, the experience can be transcending. I have walked into a worship gathering hurting deep inside and by the second or third song I can feel the healing breath of God being breathed back into my soul.

In my early days of faith, I remember many a Sunday walking into the local church to which I belonged for a worship gathering feeling like the world was going to collapse on top of me. I would sit down and scan the others there and wonder if any of them were hurting as bad as I was.

One particular Sunday, I saw a person break down and cry as the first song began. Their head fell into their hands and I could see their lungs heaving as they cried out to God. The amazing thing was their transformation over the next several songs. I don't know what was going on in their life, but they obviously had an experience with a living, loving God who breathed life back into their bones.

Giving

> John 3:16 "For God loved the world so much that he gave his one and only Son, so that everyone who believes in him will not perish but have eternal life."

"For God loved the world so much that he gave...." God is love[55] and the very essence of love is manifested by giving sacrificially. Love manifested by sacrificial giving was demonstrated by God's gift of His Son to the world.

When you give you are identifying with the very nature of God which is love. Giving breaks the chains of the antithesis of love which is selfishness; giving is like getting pure oxygen pumped into your soul.

I understand why people do not give, it is scary. We comfort ourselves by saying things like, "Someday,

---

[55] 1 John 4:8 But anyone who does not love does not know God, for God is love.

I'll have enough and then I will give big." This line of thinking may help us sleep at night, but unfortunately, we are just lying to ourselves. I had a friend who used to say, "You are playing the fools game and the only person you are foolin' is yourself."

The sad reality is if you are not faithful with a little you will not be faithful with a lot. Take one of the richest men in the world in the 20th century, John D. Rockefeller when he replied to the question by a reporter, "How much money is enough?" he said, "Just a little bit more."

True love is not giving out of your abundance, but giving out of your need. King David understood this when he told Araunah (when he tried to give David an offering that he could give to God), "I will not present an offering that has cost me nothing!"[56]

A gift of sacrifice changes the recipient and the giver. When you give sacrificially, you will never be closer to the heart and mind of Christ in this world.

Serving

> *1 Peter 4:10 God has given each of you a gift from his great variety of spiritual gifts. Use them well to serve one another.*

Like giving, serving turns on the oxygen to your soul. You make a direct connection with Jesus when you serve others. It was something that He wanted us to

---

[56] 1 Chronicles 21:24

understand and put in to practice, so much so that He modeled it in His life and made it a central theme of his ministry.[57]

As followers of Christ, we need to do just that, follow his example and the example he exemplified was that of a servant leader. Jesus could have demanded to be served, however His purpose was to equip, encourage, and edify His followers to serve others.

Every person has something to offer. You can do something someone else cannot; you were entrusted with a personality or skill that can make a positive difference in someone's life.

I do not believe your skills, personality, or even the people in your life are an accident. There is a reason God has composed a symphony that is your life, each part intertwined with the other brought together to create music that inspires the world to be better because you are in it.

SPIRITUAL EXCELLENCE:

What is spiritual excellence?

For me, I would define spiritual excellence as pursuing being fully human. In other words relentlessly pursuing a transformational relationship with your Creator; living a life that is woven with His love and grace.

---

[57] Matthew 20:28 For even the Son of Man came not to be served but to serve others and to give his life as a ransom for many."

Determining your SQ (spiritual quotient) can be done be assessing how tightly you cling to the rights of your life. A person who has a low SQ will demand autonomy and little authority in their life when it comes to God. While a person who has a high SQ will release their claim on the right to dictate the direction of their life and submit to the vision God has for them.

In order to achieve a higher SQ we need to be willing to drop the familiar chains of societal expectation which has incarcerated us and step into the wide open spaces of grace. Again, spiritual excellence does not mean perfection in living out the vision God has for your life, but it does mean that you will not settle for a common life and we will have an eagerness to exist in a new unexpected paradigm.

"Excellence is a gift; be generous."

Group Swim

breathe

Group Swim
Section 3:
Soul

Jump In:

(You can't swim unless you are in the water. The "Jump In" is an "ice breaker" question to get the group talking.)

How would you explain a soul to someone who has never heard of it?

Drill Set:

(Drills in swimming are used to improve speed and efficiency. Studying scripture in the same way refines the heart, soul, and mind to help us live out the vision God has for our life.)

Read: Genesis 2:7, Psalm 104:30, Isaiah 42:5, and Acts 17:25

What does God's breath result in according to Genesis 2:7?

Read: Psalm 57:4

If God's breath brings life, what is the meaning of Psalm 57:4?

Read: Psalm 63:1

Have you ever felt like David in this Psalm?

What was the situation where you felt like you were in "parched and weary land?"

How long were you in this place?

How did you experience God again?

Read: Psalm 25

This has been one of the most powerful psalms in my life. I especially connect with the ESV's wording in the first couple of lines, "To you O Lord, I lift up my soul. O my God, in you I trust; let me not be put to shame; let not my enemies exult over me."

Have you ever had to lift up your soul because you were spiritually on your back?

How can someone put all their trust in God?

Have you ever asked God not to let you be put to shame or have your enemies triumph over you?

Open Water Swim:

(An open water swim is the real deal, no walls to hold onto, plastic lane lines to keep people from bumping into you, or black lines painted on the bottom to keep you going in the right direction. This section is a suggestion for the participants in your group to go out and put into practice the scripture that was studied.)

Breathe in God through reading scripture, prayer, musical worship, giving, and serving. Schedule to do these things each day this week.

part 4
Navigate
loving God with all your mind

chapter eleven

OPEN WATER

"The gateway to life is very narrow and the road is difficult, and only a few ever find it."
-Jesus[58]

Open water swimming is vastly different than swimming in the controlled environment of a lap pool. In a lap pool you swim along in crystal clear water, with plastic lane markers to keep you from veering off course and a straight black line painted on the bottom of the pool to guide you to the wall, a mere 25 yards away. Swimming lap after lap can be a really mind-numbing experience because it is, well, mindless.

How different is the open water?

---

[58] Tyndale House Publishers. (2004). *Holy Bible : New Living Translation*. (2nd ed.) (Mt 7:14). Wheaton, Ill.: Tyndale House Publishers.

The open water is very rarely crystal clear. There are no lane markers to keep you going in the right direction. Even if you could see the bottom, I can assure you that nothing is painted on it to help lead you to your destination. And how far is that destination? Probably not 25 meters; sometimes, in fact, you're miles away from the shore. Compound this with current, wind, waves, and thousands of other swimmers bumping into you, and the open water situation is the antithesis of logging in laps. Outside the amenities of the lap pool, you must engage your mind and navigate if you want any hope of getting to your destination.

A few strategies are popular when it comes to open water navigation. One is going on your instinct or feeling; the wing and a prayer swim. Another is drafting off a more experienced swimmer –trusting that they know where they are going and that they have picked the best line to get there. Third is the pack approach: trying to hang in with a group and making sure you have people on the left and right of you. Finally, there's heads up swim, where you simply pick up your head every few strokes, assess where you are, and make adjustments to keep on course.

(NOT) TRUE NORTH

Navigating by instinct may feel right, but I can tell you from experience that going with my gut has a turned a lot of 1.5 mile swims into 2+ mile swims in a hurry. The truth is that our internal compass is really lousy. That's why people who can't read nature's signs of direction get hopelessly lost.

This truth was really crystallized for me by an illustration provided by Dave Ramsey.[59] He had his audience close their eyes, spin around a couple of times, and then point to north. When they opened their eyes they found people pointing in every direction. Without external help, humans do not have the innate ability to consistently go in the right direction.

Our lack of a reliable internal compass is not constrained to swimming or navigating from point A to point B, but also in our quest to navigate to a rich and satisfying life. The reality is we are exactly who we desire to be; our job, economic status, influence, body composition, relationships, education, and life are all a result of what we truly desire.

For example, a man might say he desires to have a great relationship with his kids, but when he compares family time with the time he spends working and golfing, and working on his golfing, the numbers don't add up. The truth evidenced is his desire to do other things overshadows his desire to be with his kids. Or, another man might say he desires to be thin, but the truth evidenced is his desire to watch TV and eat bloomin' onions outweigh his desire to exercise and be thin.

True desires are the ones that we live out, not the ones we state. We are a sum total of our real desires that manifest themselves in our actual life experience.

---

[59] Dave Ramsey is a conservative financial teacher who bases his advice on the Bible. www.daveramsey.com

SWING OR SHARPEN?

Last summer I drove over four thousand miles, visiting seven churches in five states, and met with fourteen pastors, I was seeking wisdom, insight, and council for leading Element3 (the church I pastor). Along the way, I heard a great story from Erwin McManus (Mosaic Church) about two lumberjacks, who had made it to the finals in a tree chopping contest. Both men were around 6'2" and 200 pounds; they both had risen to the top of this international contest by their years of experience and skill in the craft of lumberjacking.

When the big day came, hundreds of fans came to cheer on the two men in their quest to be recognized as the world's best lumberjack. Two trees had been carefully selected for the day's contest; both were equal in the size and close enough to each other for the fans to see how their favorite lumberjack was faring against his competition. When the gun went off, to signal the beginning of the competition, both men swung their mighty axes into the trunk of the trees. Thump, thump, thump as each swing cut deeper into the trees. Seconds turned into minutes as both men dug deep within themselves to stave off exhaustion in order to be the first to see their tree fall in victory.

Part way into the competition one of the men retracted his ax and then to the amazement of the crowd and his competitor, he walked away from the tree. While he walked away with his ax gently resting on his shoulder, a wave of jeers filled the air sounding their disapproval. The other lumberjack seeing his opportunity swung his ax harder and harder to eliminate any chance of his competitor ever catching up to him. No one knew where the other man had gone, but it did not matter to the crowd as they cheered louder and louder for the lumberjack, now pouring out sweat, as he continued to pound away at the resilient trunk.

After what seemed an eternity, the retreating lumberjack returned to the base of his tree and resumed swinging his ax. The crowd mocked him and yelled, "It's too late; you have lost." The returning lumberjack paid no attention, just continued swinging away. To the crowd's surprise, after a few minutes, the returning lumberjack began to catch up. Each swing of his ax brought him closer to the obviously tiring leader.

The crowd took note that the leader's ax seemed to cause blunt damage to the tree, while the returned lumberjack's ax cut cleanly and deeply into the base of the tree with every swipe. Whispers started to ripple through the crowd; some were claiming that they heard grinding metal during the time that the lumberjack was apparently retreating. Others remarked how his blade looked new compared to the laboring leader's ax. Everyone had an opinion, the excitement had reached a fevered pitch, but suddenly with a loud crack and a shout of, "Timber!" the crowd was silenced. When the dust had settled it was apparent who had won; the lumberjack who had taken the time to sharpen his blade.

This story really resonated with me because often we are so focused on *moving forward we don't* take the time to ask if *how* we are doing it is the best way. Time spent preparing or refining is as important as doing. The trick is getting the ratios right. Some spend too much time preparing to live the life God has envisioned for them, while others spend too much time living their own way and settling for less than God had envisioned for them.

AWKWARD

The most cumbersome navigation technique in open water swimming is to pick up your head every few strokes, assess where you are, and make adjustments to keep on course. While this does wreak havoc on your stroke, it also keeps you going in the correct direction without relying on your internal compass, blindly drafting off someone in front of you, or hanging in the pack with the hope you will just end up in the right place along with everyone else.

Picking up your head requires discipline and the willingness to sacrifice short term comfort and perceived progress for the hope of something better on the horizon. If we're honest, we'll admit that most of don't pick up our heads very often. Usually we are ascribing to the gut feeling approach or the pack mentality, or drafting those we think might happen to know where they're going. These are widely accepted, "normal," "ordinary" approaches to live life. There is just one problem with this. We were not created to live a normal, predictable, and ordinary life. We were created to live an extraordinary life.

You are a masterpiece created as a gift to the world, unique in purpose, and a conduit of God's love and mercy to those who are desperate for an experience with their Creator. You have been chosen to be an ambassador of Christ and a light in this dark world. Unfortunately, most people will never pick up their head in order to navigate to the life God has envisioned for them to live.

PICKING UP YOUR HEAD

Picking up your head is the practice of knowing where you are headed, taking the time to assess where you are, and making the course corrections necessary to get to your destination. In theory it seems simple enough, but the real life application of understanding your direction, actually blocking off time in your crowded calendar to assess where you are, and having the courage to make the necessary changes are extremely difficult to execute in our day-to-day struggles.

Many of us have drifted into the life we live today. Most of us did not intentionally set out to be in the job, city, and maybe even the relationships that we are currently in. It's all very innocent; we make a decision that seems right at the time, and before we know it we are stuck doing, living, or being with a job, city, or people we never thought were going to make up our life.

That is why many people experience a mid-life crisis; they wake up one day, look in the mirror and realize that they have dedicated most of their life doing something they never intended to be their life's work. Essentially, they pick up their head, look around – and find they have no idea where they are or how they got there. Terrified, they frantically try to make a change from the pursuit of status (or the status quo) to a life of significance.

This eventual picking up of our head is what makes us human; the very fact that we desire to have significance in our world sets us apart from the rest of creation. For me it is the primary evidence of God. The desire for significance has no benefit in the evolutionary scheme; it does not increase our chances to procreate or secure more food. Quite the contrary, the quest for significance is an exercise in sacrifice. Sacrificing for those who are not as well equipped to succeed in life, sacrificing for the something beyond us – and it makes room for us to experience a better life.

Can you imagine a shark or a lion making the conscious decision to sacrifice for the benefit of another? Of course not! It would have absolutely no benefit to their ability to eat or procreate. But God put something inside of us, something as ancient as Him: His likeness.[60]

A lot has been said about what attributes the "likeness of God" entails, but to me it seems His likeness may be our ability to consciously choose. Our unique human ability to think through and make decisions – to navigate our lives, choosing self or self-sacrifice, the ordinary or the extraordinary.

---

[60]"Then God said, 'Let us make human beings in our image, to be like us.'" Genesis 1:26 (NLT).

ASSESSING WHERE YOU ARE

Once you *pick up your head* you need to assess where you are and where you need to go. It is not enough just to look around. You need to take the time to process where you really are in life and determine what is your best course of action, the means of moving toward your destination. Not taking the time to do these regular life assessments may be one of the biggest mistakes people make in their lives.

In order to do a life assessment you need to take some time out of your normal busy schedule and give yourself space to just be. This should be done daily, weekly, monthly, and annually, consisting of periods of different duration and scope based on the regularity of the life assessment.

For instance a daily assessment may just be a few minutes each day in focused prayer asking God to give your clarity and direction for you to live out His vision for your life. Your weekly assessment may include going to church and dedicating the whole day to things of God and family. Your monthly assessment may be a weekend getaway with some extended time set aside to just be quiet in the presence of God. Your annual assessment could be a whole week, where you reset your priorities and make sure your life is about holistically loving God and people.

If a pilot is just a few degrees off while flying from LA to London, he could end up with some rather unhappy passengers standing in an airport in Paris. In a similar way, these regular assessments of our life are of vital importance; if you are just a few degrees off course you may end up in an unintended place. It can seem so small and insignificant at the time, but over the long journey of life even a few degrees could make us miss some of the gifts God has in store for us.

ESAU & JACOB

I heard a phenomenal talk at the 2010 Catalyst Conference by Andy Stanley on a familiar verse from the Old Testament. Stanley's premise was that God's introduction of Himself to Moses as "the God of your father—the God of Abraham, the God of Isaac, and the God of Jacob"[61] may be the most important scripture in the Bible. Pastor Stanley argued that this self-description serves to remind us that we can so easily miss the eternal for the easy, immediate or temporal decision.

I have heard this scripture taught many times, but have never really understood the power of it until Andy Stanley unpacked it at the conference. The backdrop of the significance of this scripture is found in *Genesis 25:29–34*. The scripture tells the story of two brothers named Esau and Jacob.

Esau was the first born son of the family; in the ancient Near East culture, the first born son had privileged rights. The firstborn son was entitled to two to three times the inheritance of the other sons. He was ultimately intended to be in charge of the family. Finally, and perhaps greatest of all, he received a special blessing from the father on his life. Clearly, being the first born son came with major privileges

---

[61] Exodus 3:6

and was something of great value to be treasured and protected.

THE RIGHT BOWL OF STEW

Now, like Jacob I have an older brother, and there are certain universal dynamics between an older brother and a younger brother. The predominant dynamic is simple: the older brother does not need the younger brother. As the younger brother, I always wanted to hang out with my brother and his friends, but, as you might guess, I was more of a pest than anything else.

So, you can imagine that on the rare occasion when the older brother needs something from a younger brother, the younger brother has to make the most out of the rare opportunity. I am not saying it is right, I am just saying that when it comes to the old/younger brother dynamic, the younger brother rarely has the upper hand.

One day when Jacob was cooking some stew, Esau arrived home from the wilderness exhausted and hungry. Esau said to Jacob, "I'm starved! Give me some of that red stew!"
So, when Esau came to Jacob needing something from his younger brother, it was a big deal for Jacob and he was going to milk it for all its worth.

"All right," Jacob replied, "but trade me your rights as the firstborn son."

So, here we have Jacob shooting for the stars. On the surface it does not seem like anyone in their right mind would make such a trade. Think about it, would you trade wealth, power, and God's special blessing for a *bowl of stew*?

You probably answered, "No." Of course you'd never be that foolish, right? Right . . . ?

Well, I think you would. And not only do I think *you* would, I think *I* would – in the right circumstances and for the right bowl of stew.

IMPACT MAGNIFYING & FOCALISM

So what are the right circumstances and the right bowl of stew? It is different for all of us. For some, we would trade our career, our authority, and our reputation for the arms of another who is not our spouse. For others we would trade it all for fame. It really does not matter what the *bowl of stew* is, the truth is that we all have a deep-seated darkness that could manifest itself in the right moment and for the right "reward."

Science has two words for this phenomenon; Impact Magnifying and Focalism.

Impact Magnifying is just that, the magnification of the perceived positive impact that a certain person, place or thing will do to satisfy our appetite. For example, a man thinks if he drives this car then he will be happy, or if he has this person in his life then he will be complete.

Focalism is similar to Impact Magnification; however, instead of the magnification of the importance of a person, place, or thing it is the focus of all one's energy on obtaining one's desire, to the detriment of everything else. All of us have witnessed this at some time or other in unhealthy relationships, where someone's focus on the significant other allows aspects of their life to fall to the wayside.

So, when Esau says, "Look, I'm dying of starvation! [...] What good is my birthright to me now?" he is falling victim to Impact Magnification and Focalism. He is thinking that this *bowl of stew* is going to have a bigger impact in his life than in it really is. He is focusing on the *bowl of stew* to the detriment of everything else, including his coveted birthright.

Well, in reality, he was not starving and what good was his birthright? I don't know, Esau, maybe the value of your birthright is that you get two to three times the inheritance of all your siblings, you get to be in charge, and you get a special blessing from your father. That might be kind of "good."

Unfortunately for Esau, he is in the right circumstance for the right *bowl of stew*, to give up everything that is important in his life.

THE GOD OF ~~ESAU~~ JACOB

> But Jacob said, "First you must swear that your birthright is mine." So Esau swore an oath, thereby selling all his rights as the firstborn to his brother, Jacob.

I wish I could travel back in time, to intervene on behalf of Esau. I would urge him to assess where he is, to measure the trade. Would it move him closer to God and people, or farther away? I wish I could tell him what we know in retrospect, that he had no idea what God had in store for him.

If Esau had never made this foolhardy deal, when God revealed Himself to Moses, He would have said that he was the God of Abraham, the God of Isaac, and the God of *Esau*. The privileged son would not have written himself out of this pivotal role in the history of God's grace. And for what? A bowl of stew?

Of course we cannot go back in time, we cannot interrupt that myopic deal. The reality is, if Esau would have assessed the wisdom before making this pledge, he would not have traded his legacy, his influence, his inheritance, and his authority for temporary fulfillment.

WHAT GOD HAS IN STORE

*Then Jacob gave Esau some bread and
lentil stew. Esau ate the meal, then got up
and left.*

Esau left and he had no idea how much that *bowl of stew* cost him. He thought he knew, but he had no idea.

As absurd as this story seems, we are subject to the same forces that Esau was overcome by. We lose sight of the fact that the most important things in life are having a right relationship with God and a right relationship with people. *Everything else is just a bowl of stew.*

The truth is, we also have no idea what God has in store for us. We do not know what the future holds. That is why we need to put protections in place to prevent us from trading our future for what is in front of us today. One of these protections is regular assessments of our position.

For those of us who are married, that other person will not fulfill us and make us happy. That car will not make us feel any better about ourselves. Being a little bit faster or being able to jump a little bit higher is not worth neglecting our families. Making a few more dollars or getting that promotion at work is not worth your soul.

We're all in danger of needing a time travel intervention. The temptations of Impact Magnification and Focalism require that we really know where we are and where we're headed. We need to have people in our lives who have the relational right to speak truth to us during those times, to help us actively navigate toward the finish line.

chapter twelve

COURSE CORRECTION

Solid assessment of your position and determining the action required to move toward your destination means nothing without making an actual course correction.

I read an interesting article the other day about how 90% of people who have had a coronary artery bypass do not follow through with the prescribed life change instructed by their doctor.[62] It's a hard statistic to swallow: 90% of people who made a solid assessment of their life situation, who knew they were suffering serious health complications and had even undergone a lifesaving surgery, did not ultimately follow through on the changes necessary to live a long and healthy life.

These coronary artery bypass patients are not statistical anomalies. They're human nature on

---

[62] DEUTSCHMAN, ALAN Change or Die,
http://www.fastcompany.com/magazine/94/open_chang
e-or-die.html May, 1st 2005. accessed 12/1/2010

statistical display. These patients are given "a new lease on life," a second chance to get things right, but 90% of them disregard this second chance and return to lifestyle that led to their demise in the first place.

Pattern of life is a powerful force. If a massive majority of people who had the wakeup call of bypass surgery cannot make the necessary life course correction, what makes us think we can incorporate positive life change in our life? The answer is not in the 90%, but in the 10%. If even a small percent of people are successful in making positive life change, then you can be one of that successful number. Clearly you are seeking out change in some form or fashion; after all, you're reading this book.

The process of asking hard questions, challenging assumptions, looking at scripture from new angles, gauging your current path, is all part of the process of picking up your head and making life assessment. But these acts alone do not result in life change; real life change requires follow through. Pattern of life is a powerful force – and that will prove to be a positive thing, so long as you pursue a new pattern of life, one that moves you closer to the life God has envisioned for you.

THE 10%

This means that anyone who belongs to Christ has become a

new person. The old life is gone; a
new life has begun![63]

Being a new person in Christ means that you are no longer held captive to your brokenness, hurt, or previous pattern of life.[64] Your freedom has been purchased at a high price, higher than anyone could possibly imagine, but most of us struggle to live out our freedom.[65] For some reason we continue to go back to the things that are self-destructive and prohibit us from living out the vision that God has for our lives. I believe that there are active steps you can incorporate into your life that will enable you to experience this new life.

Don't Quit. Start: Quitting things does not work long term. When you quit, you leave a void in your life that needs to be filled with something else. Unfortunately, that *something* is usually not something *productive* or *useful* in your life. So, instead of quitting, start

---

[63] 2 Co 5:17 (NLT)

[64] Romans 7:6 (NLT) "But now we have been released from the law, for we died to it and are no longer captive to its power. Now we can serve God, not in the old way of obeying the letter of the law, but in the new way of living in the Spirit."

[65] 1 Corinthians 6:20 (NLT) ". . . for God bought you with a high price. So you must honor God with your body."

something *productive* and *useful* that will crowd out that negative habit or pattern of life that is holding you back.

Work Toward a Dream: A dream can be anything in the future that would require working toward. There is something powerful about a dream. It gets us up in the morning and compels us to keep moving forward.

Do Something Every Day: Even the smallest forward motion over time equals completion. You can't run a marathon in one stride; it takes a commitment to take one more step after another until you cross the finish line. If you want to get a degree, take at least one class a semester. If you want to publish a book, write at least a sentence every day. Small steps equal long term success.

Kinetic Community: Be with people who are moving toward your dream. Your mom was right, when she said, "You are who you hang out with." Peer pressure is real so, choose your friends wisely and be around people who are moving in the direction you want to go.

Invest in others: Investing in others, who are on the same path, but not quite as far along, is one of the best ways to keep you moving forward. When people are looking to you for answers, motivation, or direction their confidence in you will inspire you to keep moving forward.

Mile Markers: Marking progress is essential in your journey. It does wonders for your motivation to hit tangible goals along the way to your ultimate destination. If you are sitting on the coach and want to run a marathon, sign up for a 5K. Having victories along the way helps you know you are making progress.

Have a Plan: Make a plan and stick to it. When you are working toward a goal, many days you just won't feel like taking the next step. Your mind can play all sorts of tricks on you to stop forward motion. The best way to overcome this temptation is make a plan on how you are going to get from where you are to where you want to be and commit to it, regardless of how you feel about it in the moment.

Remove Failure: Failure is out there, but you don't need to invite it into your house. For example, if you are trying to lose weight, you do not need to have your favorite ice cream in the house. Your home should be a safe zone to help you reach your goals.

Be Public: Telling others your plan is a great motivator. We don't tell people because if we don't succeed we do not want them to think we are losers. But, ironically, by not telling the people we respect we are setting ourselves up for failure.

Saturate: Read, watch, and listen to things that reinforce your goal. Being exposed to other people's journeys is a great way to find inspiration, direction, and communities that will help you achieve your dreams. There are magazines out there for just about everything, websites for every passion, and social clubs for everything under the sun. There have never been so many resources to help you reach your dream; so saturate yourself.

PROBLEMATIC NAVIGATION TECHNIQUES

As I mentioned in the previous chapter, many common or popular navigation approaches will inevitably lead us astray. Two of those, drafting and the pack mentality, deserve further discussion as their prevalence, potential pitfalls, and, yet, occasional usefulness is worth unpacking.

Drafting: Drafting can be a very powerful tool that enables us to concentrate on moving forward rather than trying to figure out which way is the right way to go. Drafting also reduces the effort required to cover the same amount of distance, so it is also an effective way to save your energy or move at a faster pace than you would be able to on your own.

The biggest trick is to know who to draft. If you draft off someone who is navigating by instinct or feeling you may be moving faster or with less effort toward a destination you don't want to go. Or, if they are simply too fast, you won't be able to maintain the pace. Sometimes we are following someone who is too slow, resulting in stunted paces and missed goals. Drafting the right person can take you to farther and faster than you could on your own, but draft the wrong person and you will be worse off.

In life, who you draft/follow is extremely important to your future. It is hard to know who to trust and who is going to help you live out the life that God has envisioned for you. Track record is one way to determine if someone is worthy of following. Do they have a life you want to emulate? Do they have a track record of loving God and loving people? Are they willing to pull you along and make sure you can keep in their draft? Leading and following is a difficult relationship to balance, it takes both parties to look out for the other; the leader making sure not to drop the follower and the follower making sure they do not slow down the leader. While having someone to draft behind is a blessing, ultimate responsibility for your life journey is yours.

Pack Mentality: This may seem like the safest navigation technique because you are not relying on your feelings, you are not committed to following one person, and you just hang out with everyone else and play the odds that everyone can't be wrong. After all, for those of you who are "U.S.Americans" it may all seems very democratic and can give you a sense of security knowing that, if the pack is headed in the wrong direction at least you are all headed in the wrong direction together.

There is one major problem with this line of thinking; even if you have the comfort of knowing that you are in the same boat with everyone who has headed in the wrong direction, you are still headed in the wrong direction. So, it does not matter if there are others with you to keep you company if you end up in the wrong place.

Jesus put navigating through life using the pack mentality like this, "Enter through the narrow gate because the gate and road that lead to destruction are wide. Many enter through the wide gate. But the narrow gate and the road that lead to life are full of trouble. Only a few people find the narrow gate.[66] Earlier we talked about how we are to race in a way to win the prize; Jesus reiterates that navigating with the pack leads to destruction and not to victory in Him.

INTELLECTUAL EXCELLENCE

What is intellectual excellence?

Intellectual excellence is being an intentional, lifelong learner. To be a lifelong learner you need to dedicate yourself to the discipline of proactively seeking knowledge. Read, take classes, be involved in topical discussion groups, pursue available avenues of learning.

A recent MSNBC Poll found that one out of four adults in the U.S.A. did not even read one book last year.[67] Charles Jones famously said, "You will be the same person in five years as you are today except for

---

[66] Matthew 7:13–14

[67] http://www.msnbc.msn.com/id/20381678/

the people you meet and the books you read."[68] If we're not reading, actively seeking to take in new knowledge, then we're in trouble.

Intellectual stagnation is common and expected; it is normal, ordinary. And it is not excellent. In order to be intellectually excellent you need to make a commitment to stop wasting time on things that do not increase your knowledge and understanding of God and His creation and start investing your mind time in things that will illuminate and promote elevated thinking.

"Excellence is a gift; be generous."

---

[68] *Jones, Charles "Tremendous"*,
http://quotationsbook.com/author/3862/

Group Swim

navigate

Group Swim
Section 4
Mind

Jump In:

(You can't swim unless you are in the water. The "Jump In" is an "ice breaker" question to get the group talking.)

Who was your favorite teacher growing up?

Why did you like that person so much?

Who has taught you the most in your life?

Who do you learn from now?

Drill Set:

(Drills in swimming are used to improve speed and efficiency. Studying scripture in the same way refines the heart, soul, and mind to help us live out the vision God has for our life.)

Read: Romans 7:23-25

Have you ever been at war in your mind?

What kinds of things do you do battle against in your mind?

Do you relate to the Apostle Paul's struggle with the desire to obey and the pull of your flesh?

Read: 1 Corinthians 2:16

What does it mean to have the mind of Christ?

How does one go about pursuing having the mind of Christ?

How active are you is these practices?

Read: Isaiah 32:6, proverbs 14:7, Proverbs 28:26 and Titus 3:9

What do these scriptures tell us about teaching and teachers?

Have you ever been fooled by a teacher?

How did you realize that particular teacher was wrong?

How did you handle the situation?

Would you say you have foolish or wise people influencing you in your life?

Open Water Swim:

(An open water swim is the real deal, no walls to hold onto, plastic lane lines to keep people from bumping into you, or black lines painted on the bottom to keep you going in the right direction. This section is a suggestion for the participants in your group to go out and put into practice the scripture that was studied.)

Seek out wise teachers, either in person, by book, video, or blogs. Fill your mind with God's wisdom.

part 5
Kick
loving God with all your strength

"First is balance. Your upper body and your legs should share the effort of moving you through the water. Specifically, your arms should make a 50 percent to 70 percent contribution to your forward propulsion while your legs should account for the remaining 50 percent to 30 percent. Swimmers who drag their legs behind their body, with almost no visible kick, are missing out on the potential core power that is derived from the hips."

-Sara McLarty

I have a weak kick. I don't think I should, but I do. In fact it is so bad that I can hardly make it across the pool with a kickboard. I have worked at it, but to this day I can still hear the snickers from my fellow swimmer friends as I labor across the pool. (While the actual snickers may be in my head, it's embarrassing all the same.)

I have received all sorts of advice from well-meaning coaches, friends, and family about how to improve my kick, but to this day it is the weak link in my swimming. I even had one friend suggest that I stop kicking altogether, because he thought I was doing more harm than good. This weak kick subsequently, throws off my balance and reduces my potential forward propulsion by as much as 30% to 50%.

For many people, the *kick* (loving God with all your strength) is the weak link in their pursuit to holistically loving God and loving people. They struggle with their diet, they find it hard to find time to exercise, and as a result they are overweight, out of shape, and physically hampered in their desire to serve God and others.

Like smokers, people who are overweight and out of shape have good intentions to get healthy, but it never seems like they can find something that works for the long haul.

I read a disturbing statistic the other day; according to the United States federal government officials, 25.6% of Americans are obese.[69] But, I thought, that's Americans, not American Evangelical Christians. Surely, Evangelical Christians who claim an adherence to the word of God would demonstrate a

---

[69] 11. Department of Health and Human Services *Healthy People 2010* (conference ed, in 2 vols). (Washington DC: US Department of Health and Human Services; 2000. Available at: http://www.health.gov/healthypeople).

commitment to God's instruction by treating their body as a temple?[70] Unfortunately, a study by Ken Ferraro of Purdue University published in *The Journal for the Scientific Study of Religion*, found that 27% of Evangelicals are obese.[71]

Just to be clear, there are a greater percentage of obese American Evangelical Christians than there are obese Americans.

This blows me away, because you would anticipate that Evangelicals would comply with Paul's teaching in Romans 12:2:

"Don't copy the behavior and customs of this world, but let God transform you into a new person by changing the way you think. Then you will learn to know God's will for you, which is good and pleasing and perfect."[72]

I would think that those who take such words to heart would demonstrate a different way of life through the way they live. On the contrary, not only have Evangelicals copied the behaviors and customs of our world, but they have surpassed them by 1.4%!

---

[70] 1 Corinthians 6:19–20 (NLT) [19] "Don't you realize that your body is the temple of the Holy Spirit, who lives in you and was given to you by God? You do not belong to yourself, [20] for God bought you with a high price. So you must honor God with your body."

[71] www.wiley.com/bw/journal.asp?ref=0021-8294

[72] Romans 12:2 (NLT)

AN ANCIENT HERESY

One of the unexpected consequences of the Industrial Revolution appears to be that it ushered in a new era of distorted Docetism.[73] It is not that modern Christians necessarily view physical matter as evil; it is probably more accurate to say that many modern Christians' actions hold the view that one's physical body is inconsequential in the grand scheme of God's eternal plan. One example of this act of neglect is evidenced by the epidemic of obesity in the Evangelical American church.

OUT OF BALANCE

When we do not feel well physically, our heart, soul, mind and love for others suffer. This is not theory or a hypothesis derived from esoteric research; this is a truth everyone has experienced.

When people are sick or injured they often lack the patience and compassion they naturally have when they are healthy. The parallels of our emotional

---

[73] Docetism [dŏsʹə tĭzʹəm]. An early teaching, regarded as heretical, according to which Christ's incarnation (i.e., taking human form) was only a matter of appearance (Gk. dokéō "seem"). Docetism is related to a gnostiic view of an irreconcilable conflict between two eternal principles — the spiritual (or good) and the material (or evil) — a conflict which precludes the possibility of the Son of God ever assuming human (i.e., material) form.

and physical condition can hardly be overstated. Think about it: How were you feeling physically during the times in your life when you were the most compassionate, generous, loving? Most of the time we find that our positive physical state allowed for or promoted our emotional wellbeing. Our physical health is crucial to our emotional, spiritual, and intellectual health.

There is a beautiful young lady in our church who used to be overweight to the point that she needed to use a cane to get around. She used most of her energy just walking from point A to point B. The physical drain was also a direct social and emotional drain.

A year and a half ago, she began having a holy discontentment with her state of physical health. She decided that she was going to make the adjustments necessary to become her healthy weight.

It was so exciting seeing her come into the worship gathering each week and tracking her progress via Facebook. It was encouraging seeing her posts about the new and healthy recipes she was cooking for her family. It was a joyful victory we celebrated with her the first time she was able to walk in without her cane.

The most triumphant moment of her journey from my perspective, however, occurred in an economically distressed area of our city, where we deliver groceries to under-resourced families and help repair homes. I remember walking up to the park where people from our church play with the neighborhood kids, when I saw her there working on a craft with one of the little girls.

What a profound triumph to witness! She had reached a place where she was physically healthy enough to be the tangible hand of Christ in a way and to a degree that months before her physical state would have denied her.

HOT DOGS AND CIGARETTES

I was at a gas station yesterday, putting some $3.10 per gallon 87 octane in my 1998 Jeep Wrangler. Instead of watching the grand total climb up on the digital display like a hyperactive chipmunk, I began looking around for something interesting to take my mind off the pain – the kind of thing I also do when I am getting a shot at the doctor's.

As a looked around my eyes finally rested on a red 20 foot banner with white words scrolling across it: "2 HOTDOGS for $1 – CIGARETTES $44.99 a CASE."

Wow! I thought to myself, *I could stop the pump a gallon early and get myself six hotdogs.* Cheap food, expensive gas, and lung cancer on sale for $45 a case. If our body is a temple for the Holy Spirit, I wonder whose temple is the typical American gas station?

You will be happy to know that I did not stop short on filling my tank with gas to buy the hotdogs. To be honest, it was not even a real temptation; it was more of an attempt at self-amusement to ease the pain at the pump. (As a pastor, I often tell young church planters when they are going through adversity that they can either laugh or cry; they get to choose.)

Although gas station hotdogs are not a temptation now, it was only seven years ago that I would not have thought twice about dropping $2 for four gas station hotdogs.

Seven years ago I did not exercise and pretty much ate whatever my stomach told me to. As a result I weighed 260 pounds, suffered a bad back, and fought the desire to take "power naps" every few hours. I loved Jesus, but I had not yet submitted that part of my life over to him.

Besides, I had all the excuses:

"I'm big boned."

"God loves me the way I am."

"My value is not based on how I look."

Or, my favorite: "I reject magazine perfection."

Good Lord, I am 6'2" and was 260 pounds – I was hardly in danger of being mistaken for an anorexic runway model.

I had completely bought into a lie disguised as the truth and, because of that, my life was out of balance and a shadow of the vision God had for me. To revisit the swimming metaphor, I had forward progress, but I was dragging my legs and losing 30% to 50% of my core power.

IT'S A LORDSHIP ISSUE

I have a friend who is in his twenties. He does not like to exercise and eats, well, like I would imagine my 10-year old son would if he were not supervised. I have tried to speak into his life about this for years, only to experience resistance to the topic.

The other day I sat down with him, shared some of God's word and expressed to him that treating his body as God's temple is a discipleship or Lordship issue. I told him that God has entrusted him with his body and he was to be a good steward of what God has given him.[74] For the first time, I felt like what I was saying was somewhat well received.

I don't think most people like to associate diet and exercise with their relationship with God, but God created the physical as much as He created the spiritual. Many times it's easier to think about God in an abstract, spiritual sense – the God who only cares about your soul – but by doing so, we deny His Lordship over all creation.

New Testament teaching elevates the importance of bringing glory to God through the physical body to the same level as heart, mind, and soul. One example of this elevation is found in 1 Corinthians 6:19-20:

---

[74] 1 Corinthians 6:19-20 Don't you realize that your body is the temple of the Holy Spirit, who lives in you and was given to you by God? You do not belong to yourself, for God bought you with a high price. So you must honor God with your body.

Don't you realize that your body is the temple of the Holy Spirit, who lives in you and was given to you by God? You do not belong to yourself, for God bought you with a high price. So you must honor God with your body.[75]

Throughout scripture we are reminded that whatever a person eats, drinks or does, indeed matters to God.[76] God instructs His creation to honor Him with their heart, mind, and soul as well as their strength because the body is interwoven with the emotions and intellect and spirit. These aspects of the self cannot be separated.[77]

While exercise is important, it is only part of the equation of loving God with all your strength; diet is also of vital importance in our overall health. The infamous city of Sodom's demise was ushered in by "pride, laziness, and gluttony, while the poor and needy suffered outside her door."[78] (More on self-indulgence while ignoring the needs of others in Section 6: Loving Others as Yourself.)

Sodom was notorious for its self-indulgent lifestyle that did not honor God, a lifestyle that

---

[75] 1 Corinthians 6:19-20 (NLT)

[76] 1 Corinthians 10:31 (NLT) "So whether you eat or drink, or whatever you do, do it all for the glory of God."

[77] 2 Corinthians 5:3 (NLT) "For we will put on heavenly bodies; we will not be spirits without bodies."

[78] Ezekial 16:49 (NLT)

eventually led to its downfall. Throughout the Bible, the importance of a God-honoring diet is emphasized in many passages, such as a particularly famous episode in Daniel, myriad articles in the Law of Moses, several verses in Proverbs, and some of the teachings of Jesus. (Ancient pagan and secular history and literature is likewise concerned with physical health. One particularly influential thinker, Hippocrates, considered to be the father of medicine, prescribed a veritable pharmacy of edibles from bread soaked in wine to boiled fish.)

YOUR AILMENT MAY BE ON YOUR FORK

An abundance of emerging research on nutrition cures demonstrates that diet can have a direct positive impact on our lives, from controlling our anxiety to preventing cancer. For example, the Reader's Digest book *Food Cures* states:

> . . . researchers have discovered, for instance, that arthritis isn't a simple case of wear and tear but rather a destructive process spurred by molecules called free radicals. This knowledge opened the door to the next discovery: that getting more leafy green and orange and yellow produce, rich in antioxidants which neutralize free radicals, helps stave off this crippling condition.[79]

---

[79] 18. The Reader's Digest Association, Inc., *Food Cures: Breakthrough Nutritional Prescriptions for everything from colds to Cancer.* (Pleasantville, New York, 2007, 12).

Researchers have shown that loving/honoring God with all your strength/body result in many physiological and psychological benefits. Such benefits help facilitate one's ability to experience a richer, more abundant life. Perhaps no greater testament to God's redemptive plan for a believer's life exists than for others to witness, and experience along with them, their rich and abundant life.

The Message puts it this way: "Live a lover's life, circumspect and exemplary, a life Jesus will be proud of: bountiful in fruits from the soul, making Jesus Christ attractive to all, getting everyone involved in the glory and praise of God."[80]

Unfortunately, poor physical health can lead to poor emotional health, and darken one's outlook on life. In a particularly nasty version of a vicious cycle, according to David Spiegel, M.D., this negative outlook can in turn directly impact our health. Spiegel says, "A lot of bad health behavior can be linked to bad emotional management."[81]

This self-propagating cycle is damaging to the heart, mind, soul, body, and one's ability to love others. This can progress in many ways. For example, people who are on a negative track seem to feel their actions and choices do not matter, often leading them to make poor food choices and resisting

---

[80] Philippians 1:10-11 (Message)

[81] Frances Lefkowitz, "Mastering The Mind Body Connection," Body and Soul Magazine (2009): 98-100.

exercise, which in turn leads to poorer health and more emotional distress – a downward spiral that is hard to reverse.

JESUS CARES ABOUT YOUR BODY

I like to ask people what Jesus' main activity was during his earthly ministry. Do you know? You may have the uncontrolled Sunday School response: "Died for our sins on the cross and rose again on the third day." Ok, that is obviously central to our faith and hope, but it was only one weekend out of his entire life. What did he do the other 33 years of his life, more specifically, the three years that are recorded in the Gospels?

If death and resurrection was his only purpose for coming to earth, then why didn't he just go straight to the cross and head promptly back to heaven? Obviously, there was more to Immanuel (God with us) than his death and resurrection. But, what was it?

Revelation.

The prevailing view of God in the first century had drifted so far from whom God really was and what He truly cared about, that Jesus came to be the very revelation of God – to the first century and all subsequent generations.[82] Religion had stolen God's

---

[82] John 14:7 (NLT) "If you had really known me, you would know who my Father is. From now on, you do know him and have seen him!"

throne and destroyed the relationship God had envisioned with his creation.[83] In other words, religious people had all the right Sunday School answers, but their hearts were far from God.[84]

But, God had a greater purpose. His purpose for coming was to reveal that God wanted more for us; he wanted to give us a rich and satisfying life. He came not for salvation alone – though certainly that is His greatest purpose – but also to reveal to us that he cares not only about the spirit, but the body and mind as well.

This is why he did not just arrive, pay for our sins, and then get out of Dodge. He wanted to give us a new way to think about our life, now and eternal. He wanted to model for us his concern for his creation's physical wellbeing in addition to the psychological and emotional and spiritual.

John 14:9 (NLT) Jesus replied, "Have I been with you all this time, Philip, and yet you still don't know who I am? Anyone who has seen me has seen the Father! So why are you asking me to show him to you?"

[83] John 10:10 (NLT) [10] "The thief's purpose is to steal and kill and destroy. My purpose is to give them a rich and satisfying life."

[84] Mark 7:6 (NLT) Jesus replied, "You hypocrites! Isaiah was right when he prophesied about you, for he wrote, 'These people honor me with their lips, but their hearts are far from me."

A MINISTRY OF HEALING

So what was Jesus' main activity during his earthly ministry? It very well may have been healing people. As far as I can tell, the Gospels record thirty-four specific healings; on top of that Matthew and Mark both record different times where Jesus healed "many" and "all" who came to him.[85] Contrast that

---

[85] Matthew 8:16–17 (NLT) "[16] That evening many demon-possessed people were brought to Jesus. He cast out the evil spirits with a simple command, and he healed all the sick. [17] This fulfilled the word of the Lord through the prophet Isaiah, who said, "He took our sicknesses and removed our diseases.""

Matthew 12:15 (NLT) "[15] But Jesus knew what they were planning. So he left that area, and many people followed him. He healed all the sick among them . . . "

Matthew 15:30 (NLT) "[30] A vast crowd brought to him people who were lame, blind, crippled, those who couldn't speak, and many others. They laid them before Jesus, and he healed them all."

Mark 1:34 (NLT) "[34] So Jesus healed many people who were sick with various diseases, and he cast out many demons. But because the demons knew who he was, he did not allow them to speak."

Mark 3:10 (NLT) "[10] He had healed many people that day, so all the sick people eagerly pushed forward to touch him."

with how many sermons are recorded that Jesus gave. One. The Sermon on the Mount.

In fairness, Jesus was not the sermon-giving type; he was more of a storyteller. So, if you include all his parables you would arrive at a total of fifty-seven, but many of those were part of the same illustration.

My purpose here is not to numerically validate a hierarchy of value; rather, it is to illustrate that Jesus deeply cared for and spent a large amount of his ministry restoring people physically. That much is undeniable.

In a discussion with a dear friend, they pushed back on this saying that the reason for Jesus' healing was to attract people to his teachings. If this is true then why did he early on in his ministry tell people he healed not to tell anyone?[86] To me this speaks to the

---

Mark 6:13 (NLT) "13 And they cast out many demons and healed many sick people, anointing them with olive oil."
[86] Matthew 8:4 (NLT) "4 Then Jesus said to him, 'Don't tell anyone about this. Instead, go to the priest and let him examine you. Take along the offering required in the law of Moses for those who have been healed of leprosy. This will be a public testimony that you have been cleansed.'"

Mark 1:44 (NLT) "44 'Don't tell anyone about this. Instead, go to the priest and let him examine you. Take along the offering required in the law of Moses for those who have been healed of leprosy. This will be a public testimony that you have been cleansed.'"

Luke 5:14 (NLT) "14 Then Jesus instructed him not to tell anyone what had happened. He said, "Go to the priest

personal nature of God. Even though he has a big stage purpose of restoring creation to Him, He still takes the time to connect and love on a personal level, off the stage and out of the lights.

---

and let him examine you. Take along the offering required in the law of Moses for those who have been healed of leprosy. This will be a public testimony that you have been cleansed.'"

chapter fourteen
RIGHT BY RESULTS

"Running long and hard is an ideal antidepressant, since it's hard to run and feel sorry for yourself at the same time. Also, there are those hours of clear-headedness that follow a long run."

-Monte Davis, runner

In the previous chapter I mentioned that I was 6'2" and once weighed 260 pounds. The story of my life was going from gimmick diet to gimmick diet. I tried low fat diets, low carb diets; I even tried a hotdog, banana, and egg diet. All of these diets helped me lose some weight at the beginning – weight which came back as soon as I (inevitably) reverted to my normal eating habits.

For the past 5+ years I have been able to sustain a healthy weight of 200 pounds. This has only been possible by accepting my body as a temple for the Holy Spirit and realizing that I am not my own. No gimmicky cheat-sheet on what to eat or a momentarily convincing dietary "revolution." It has come from a transformative understanding of who I am and *whose* I am.

But there have been some common sense, practical breakthroughs as well. A few of the more helpful I've included in this chapter.

Mark's 10 Commandments for Being Your Ideal Weight

I thought it might be helpful to pass along 10 of the most beneficial changes that assisted me in my personal transformation.

1. **Thou shalt only make sustainable changes.**

   Gimmick diets may work for the short term, but let's be honest, how long can you go only eating pork products? Before you make a change in your life ask yourself if it is sustainable for the rest of your life. If the answer is, "No," then don't do it.

2. **Thou shalt lose ounces not pounds.**

   No one loses or gains fat in pounds; we lose and gain in ounces. There are about 3,500 calories in a pound of fat. So in order to lose a pound of fat you need to have a 3,500 calorie deficit in your diet. But since no one loses pounds only ounces (16oz make a pound) let's look at what it will take to lose an ounce. If you are currently drinking 16oz of Coke a day and switched to Diet Coke (I suggest water, but remember only make sustainable change) you would lose about 1oz of fat a day. In the course of a year you would lose around 22.8 pounds. Small changes, big results.

3. **Thou shalt not eat while watching TV, movies, or surfing the computer.**

Reason: Mindless eating can easily add a 1,000 calories (5oz of fat) or so a day.

4. **Thou shalt not eat fast food.**

Processed foods like the ones you find at McDonald's are low in nutritional value and high in calories. If you are on the go, run into a supermarket and grab some turkey meat from the deli and some whole grain bread and make yourself a filling yet healthy sandwich.

5. **Thou shalt not eat out of the bag/carton.**

Portion control is critical. If you are going to eat something that is from a bag/carton, don't eat it out of the bag/carton. This includes ice cream as well (sad).

6. **Thou shalt read the label.**

Reading the label before you buy it will help you decide how you want to spend your approximately 2,000 calorie daily quota.

7. Thou shalt think through your eating.

Let's face it, 2,000 calories a day is not a whole lot. That means to get the most out of your calories you need to think through what you intend to eat for the entirety of the day. For instance a 4oz skinless chicken breast has 110 calories and a 3oz 80/20 (lean/fat) hamburger patty contains 230 calories. I don't know about you, but I would much rather have 8oz of skinless chicken breast at 220 calories than 3oz of hamburger patty (3oz, really!?) at 230 calories.

8. Thou shalt grill not fry.

Frying adds fat and calories and does not taste as good as grilling.

9. Thou shalt drink lots of H2O.

If your belly is full of water, you can't fill it with food. It also flushes your system.

10. Thou shalt move.

I can't live on 2,000 calories a day. OK, I could, but I really don't want to. So, that means something else must change. That change is movement. I am 6'2" and 200 pounds; if I run a mile I'll burn about 150 calories (Exercise Calorie Counter http://www.prohealth.com/weightloss/tools /exercise/calculator1_2.cfm). Or another way to look at it is: I get to eat another chicken breast at dinner. Simple math: If you want to eat more than 2,000 calories, you gotta move to make up the difference.

FNRP (FAT IS NOT A RESPECTER OF PERSONS)

Unless you are blessed and have an abnormality where your body does not metabolize fat,[87] you are subject to FNRP (Fat is Not a Respecter of Persons). Simply put, if you take in more calories than you burn you will gain fat. It's not personal, it's just math. A typical person will burn 2,000 calories a day without intentional exercise. If you take in more than 2,000 calories a day you will store it as fat. If you store up to 3,200 extra calories, congratulations you have gained a pound of fat. Fat does not care who you are, it's just stored energy. On the flip side, you don't need to feel bad if you burn a few extra calories. Your fat won't mind; it's not a respecter of persons.

THE E.A.R. FORMULA

To experience a physically healthy and balanced life you need to know what a healthy balance is for you.

For example the energy intake (by the way, energy is the new term for a calorie) required to fuel a marathon runner is going to be vastly different than the energy needs of a nine-to-five office worker who walks 30 minutes a day after dinner. Both can experience physical excellence, but their energy intake requirements are going to be unique to their

---

[87] http://blogs.discovermagazine.com/discoblog/2009/03/17/why-do-some-people-never-get-fat-scientists-may-have-the-answer/

activity level. This is also true of rest. The more energy you expend the more recovery/rest time you need.

I use a simple (but essential) equation for physical excellence: **E+A+R=PE**

Energy

+

Activity

+

Rest/Recovery
Physical Excellence

Formula Explained: Your Energy/Calorie Intake + Your Activity + Your Rest/Recovery must be balanced to experience Physical Excellence.

Example #1: The Marathon Runner

Let's take a marathon runner as an example. Let's say he is 180 pounds and runs 35 miles a week.

- His energy/nutrition/calorie expenditure before he does anything:
  - **2,500 Kcal** per day
- His average energy/nutrition/calorie expenditure with his running:
  - An additional **700 Kcal** per day
- This makes his total daily energy/nutrition/calorie intake requirement:
  - **3,200 Kcal** to maintain his current weight.

Our marathon runner needs to eat an average of 3,200 Kcal (energy/nutrition/calorie) per day to fuel his activity. If he eats more, he gains weight; if he eats less and he will lose weight. Simple math.

Now remember, food is energy. So, if he restricts his diet he will be using stored energy (fat) and once that is gone the body will start to feed off itself (it starts burning muscle after fat) to get the energy it needs.

Have you ever been on a low Kcal (energy/nutrition/calorie) diet and just felt tired? This is because your body was not getting the energy it needed. You may be saying, "But Mark, I have lots of stored energy!" Unfortunately, stored energy is not as easily converted into the fuel needs of the body as food.

A good rule of thumb is to not restrict more than 15% to 20% of your energy needs per day.[88] So, if our marathon runner wants to lose 1 pound (again, there are approximately 3,500 Kcal in a pound of fat) and decides to restrict his Kcal intake by 15% or a total intake of an average of 2,700 Kcal per day, then in about 7-days he will have lost 1 pound of stored energy.

---

[88] Calorie intake to lose weight http://www.bmi-calculator.net/bmr-calculator/harris-benedict-equation/calorie-intake-to-lose-weight.php

Example #2: The Walking Office Worker

Now let's use our walking office worker as an example. Let's say she is 140 pounds and walks 30 minutes a day.

- Her energy/nutrition/calorie expenditure before she does anything is:
    o **2,000 Kcal** per day.
- Her average energy/nutrition/calorie expenditure with her walking is:
    o An additional **100 Kcal** per day.
- This makes her total daily energy/nutrition/calorie intake requirement:
    o **2,100 Kcal** to maintain her current weight.

OK, let's say our walking office worker wants to drop 10 pounds, but she does not want to restrict her eating and does not have time for more than 30 minutes of exercise a day. Well, that means she needs to find an activity that burns more energy per minute. Below is a simple exercise calorie calculator (also included in "Thou shalt move") to help you determine what activity is best for you.

Exercise Calorie Calculator
http://www.prohealth.com/weightloss/tools/exercise/calculator1_2.cfm

Knowing your energy requirement takes a little effort, but your body is a temple for the Holy Spirit and if you want to experience physical excellence, it is going to take some time investment on your part.

Rest

We are a tired people. The number one answer to the question, "How are you doing?" is "Tired." Rest/Sleep/Recovery is essential in order to experience physical excellence. The more we push ourselves the more rest we need.

I hear people all the time tell me that they "get by on 5 or 6 hours of sleep a night." That is precisely right; they are only "getting by" and are not experiencing physical excellence.

In our two examples, our marathon runner is clearly going to need more rest/sleep/recovery than our walking office worker. Ultimately, it is a system of trial and error determining how much rest/sleep/recovery you need to experience physical excellence.

A good way to do this is keep a journal with your energy/calorie intake and expenditures along with how much rest you got. The next day rate how you feel on a scale of 1 to 10, before long you will begin to see how the three factors of Energy + Activity + Recovery = Physical Excellence.

PHYSICAL EXCELLENCE:

What is physical excellence?

I think the best definition of physical excellence would be a commitment to the Apostle Paul's instruction in 1 Corinthians 6:18-20 and 1 Thessalonians 4:3-5.[89] [90] In these two scriptures he talks about the dangers of sexual sin and how it affects the body, but I think it goes even farther than that. We are also instructed to be holy.

The word holy in scripture has two meanings which has been an area of confusion for many a follower of Christ. When the word holy is used in the context of God, it means absolutely pure; but when it is used in the context of people or things, it means to be set aside for God's purpose.

---

[89] 1 Corinthians 6:18–20 (NLT) Run from sexual sin! No other sin so clearly affects the body as this one does. For sexual immorality is a sin against your own body.

Don't you realize that your body is the temple of the Holy Spirit, who lives in you and was given to you by God? You do not belong to yourself, for God bought you with a high price. So you must honor God with your body.

[90] 1 Thessalonians 4:3–5 (NLT) God's will is for you to be holy, so stay away from all sexual sin. Then each of you will control his own body and live in holiness and honor— not in lustful passion like the pagans who do not know God and his ways.

So, when we are commanded to treat our bodies as holy, we are being called to set aside our bodies for God's purpose; this is the definition of physical excellence.

In the context of all scripture we are warned not only about sexual sin, but also gluttony, and drunkenness. [91] [92] Now sexual sin is not sex, gluttony is not having a big meal at Thanksgiving, and drunkenness is not having a glass of wine with dinner.

God's vision for our lives is to have a robust and passionate sexual experience with our spouse; it is part of his plan. Without the gift of sex, this book would not have been written and you would not be reading it. Unfortunately, God's creation has misused this gift and in many instances turned one of God's greatest gifts into something destructive and dark.

God is also the God of the celebration. In fact there are seven Jewish feasts where, well you get to feast.[93] Having an occasional big meal is not gluttony or sin. Where it is a problem is when overeating becomes the normal pattern of life resulting in an unhealthy weight.

---

[91] Proverbs 23:2 (NLT) If you are a big eater, put a knife to your throat;

[92] Ephesians 5:18 (NLT) Don't be drunk with wine, because that will ruin your life. Instead, be filled with the Holy Spirit,

[93] Passover Supper —The Feast of Unleavened Bread — — The Feast of First Fruits — The Feast of Pentecost — The Feast of Trumpets — The Day of Atonement —The Feast of Tabernacles.

Depending on your brand of Christianity, the next few paragraphs may make you mad.

God does not have a problem with alcohol. Wine is a central part of the Passover Seder which was the meal Jesus and his disciples were having in the upper room on the night Jesus was arrested and is also the basis of communion or the Lord's Table. This is why Paul had to correct the believers in Corinth for getting wasted at worship gatherings.[94]

Probably, the most interesting thing about Jesus and alcohol is found in John 2. This was the beginning of Jesus' earthly ministry and at this point He had not performed any public miracles.

So, Jesus was at a wedding with his friends and family and the supply of wine, that the hosts of the party thought would be enough, ran out. At this point, Jesus' mother came to Him and asked if he would fix the problem.

With a little protest about timing, Jesus then turned 120 to 180 gallons of water into wine. When the Master of Ceremonies tried it he exclaimed, "A host always serves the best wine first," he said. "Then, when everyone has had a lot to drink, he brings out the less expensive wine. But you have kept the best until now!" John 2:10

---

[94] 1 Corinthians 11:21 (NLT) For some of you hurry to eat your own meal without sharing with others. As a result, some go hungry while others get drunk.

There you have it. Jesus' first miracle was to keep the party going; sort of a divine beer run. All the wine at the party had been drunk and he did a miracle to keep the party going. No wonder after that Jesus got invited to so many parties.

Followers of Christ should treat their bodies, which are the temple for the Holy Spirit, with respect and reverence. Health is not a right – it is a gift a gift that can be misused and damaged. Be physically excellent by treating your body as something holy; something set aside for God's purpose.

"Excellence is a gift; be generous."

Group Swim

kick

Group Swim
Section 5
Strength

Jump In:

(You can't swim unless you are in the water. The "Jump In" is an "ice breaker" question to get the group talking.)

How important is fitness to you?

Do you count calories?

How many days a week do you exercise?

Drill Set:

(Drills in swimming are used to improve speed and efficiency. Studying scripture in the same way refines the heart, soul, and mind to help us live out the vision God has for our life.)

Read: 1 Corinthians 6:18–20

What does this scripture tell us about the importance of our body?

How does God view our body?

Do you believe that your view of your body is in harmony with God's view of your body?

How so or how not so?

Does your life style reflect that your body is a temple for the Holy Spirit?

178

Read: 1 Thessalonians 4:3–5

If God's will is for you to be holy (set apart for His purpose) what do you think that looks like in your everyday life?

Do you ever get mad at people for whom physical health seems comes easy?

Why does it make you feel that way?

Read: Proverbs 23:2 and Ephesians 5:18

How does God view drunkenness and gluttony?

Why is it a problem?

In light of God's view on your body, what changes do you need to make in your daily life?

Open Water Swim:

(An open water swim is the real deal, no walls to hold onto, plastic lane lines to keep people from bumping into you, or black lines painted on the bottom to keep you going in the right direction. This section is a suggestion for the participants in your group to go out and put into practice the scripture that was studied.)

Take some time and personalize the E+A+R=PE equation for your life. Make a plan to treat your body as the temple it is.

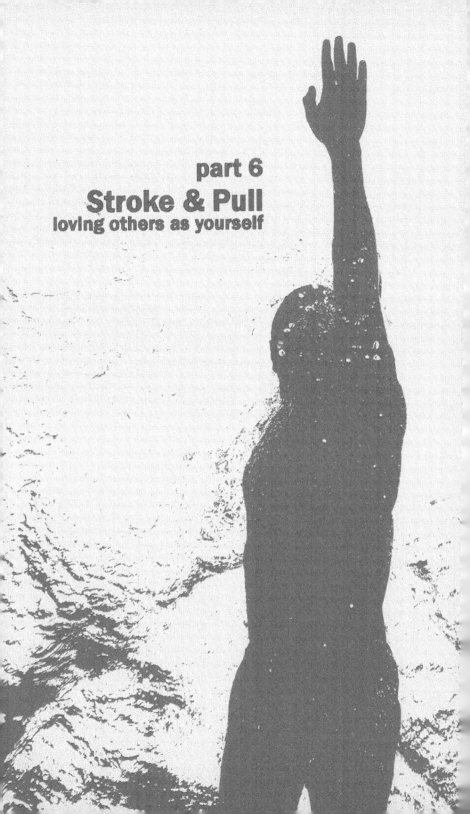

part 6
Stroke & Pull
loving others as yourself

chapter fifteen

DON'T BE A DRAG

> *"When the toe-to-head distance between two swimmers is half a meter, the trailing swimmer experiences a 45 percent reduction in drag."*
>
> -Jim Gourley

Whether it is in swimming, NASCAR, or in life having someone go ahead, forging the trail, makes it easier for the next person to move forward. John Adams said it this way:

> *"I must study politics and war that my sons may have liberty to study mathematics and philosophy. My sons ought to study mathematics and philosophy, geography, natural history, naval architecture, navigation, commerce, and agriculture, in order to give their children a right to study painting, poetry, music, architecture, statuary, tapestry, and porcelain."*

We have all benefited from those who went before us and it is the love for others that makes us intentionally help those who are to follow.

I believe one of life's highest callings is to be the tangible hand of Christ -- to be the person who reaches out and pulls someone farther than they could go on their own. This can be done in both big and small ways, publicly or privately, personally or anonymously. However you choose, the most important things is to tangibly love others in the name of Christ.

I think, in one regard, loving others in the abstract is an idea to which it is easy to yield intellectual consent. But with Jesus' addition of "as yourself," loving others is brought to an uncomfortable degree of clarity – a clarity that is quantifiable in both experience and practice.

HOW DO I LOVE ME? LET ME COUNT THE WAYS...

In my own journey to move from an abstract intellectual acceptance of "loving others," to an uncomfortable clarity that is quantifiable. I decided one day it would be helpful to make a list in my journal of how I love myself and then compare it to how I love others. The following is an excerpt from my personal journal:

- *When I am hungry, I feed myself.*
- *When I am thirsty, I get myself a drink.*
- *When I am cold, I get myself a jacket.*
- *When I am scared, I comfort myself.*
- *When I am sick, I give myself medicine.*
- *When I am lonely, I find myself fellowship.*

- *When I am bored, I entertain myself.*

One thing is for sure; no one loves me like I love me.

But, do I love others as I love myself?

- *When others are hungry . . .*
  . . . I'll sometimes feed them, but certainly not with the urgency that I feed myself.

- *When others are thirsty . . .*
  . . . I have actually helped to provide a healthy water source for a group of people in a clean water project, but that was only once. I'll gladly buy a friend a coffee, though. That counts for something, right?

- *When others are cold . . .*
  . . . I will give them one of my jackets.

- *When others are scared . . .*
  . . . If I know about it I will try to comfort them.

- *When others are sick. . .*
  . . . I will do what I can to get them medicine.

- *When others are lonely . . .*
  . . . If it's convenient I will hang out with them for a while.

- *When others are bored . . .*

...to be honest, I don't see myself as an "on-call" entertainer.

Before you judge me, I would encourage you to do the same exercise. Not that our collective failure in this area will make us feel better about ourselves, but it will give us common ground to encourage each other to move closer to the heart and mind of Christ in this matter.

In many ways, loving God with all your heart, soul, mind, and strength can be easy in comparison to loving others as yourself. The tension created by this command is increased even more by the fact that Jesus said that the command to love others as yourself is equal to his command to holistically love God.

EXPECTATION MANAGEMENT

If you struggle with loving others as yourself you are not alone. This struggle has been a constant one at the heart of believers ever since this command was first given.

Most people's initial response (including mine), to this command is management of the expectation. I have seen this management in both modern literature and in ancient texts. I don't blame anyone for trying to make this command more manageable. After all, it strikes right at the heart of our selfish nature.

One attempt of justification of one's actions is found in Luke 10:25–37:

One day an expert in religious law stood up to test Jesus by asking him this question: "Teacher, what should I do to inherit eternal life?"

Jesus replied, "What does the law of Moses say? How do you read it?"

The man answered, "You must love the Lord your God with all your heart, all your soul, all your strength, and all your mind.' And, 'Love your neighbor as yourself.'"

"Right!" Jesus told him. "Do this and you will live!"

The man wanted to justify his actions, so he asked Jesus, "And who is my neighbor?"[95]

Here we have someone who had heard Jesus' teachings and had even adopted Jesus' new interpretation of the Law of Moses into his belief system. How do I know that he had heard and adopted Jesus' teachings? Because the original command given by Moses did not include "mind." In fact "mind" was an addition by Jesus.[96] So, when the expert in religious law, who obviously knew the Law of Moses, added 'mind' we can know that he had heard

---

[95] Luke 10:25–37 (NLT)

[96] Deuteronomy 6:5 (NLT) "And you must love the LORD your God with all your heart, all your soul, and all your strength."

and accepted Jesus' teachings on an intellectual level.

Many times when I read stories like this in scripture, I am pretty quick to condemn the person who is trying to justify their own way of living, rather than committing themselves to the person and teaching of Jesus. I mean really, what follower of Christ would ever try to justify their own way of living, rather than committing themselves to the person and teaching of Jesus? Oh, wait... I do that all the time.

Thankfully, Jesus is patient and always has the goal of leading his creation into the life that he has envisioned for them. Because of that when we fall short of those thoughts, habits, and actions he would have us aspire to, he takes the time to lead us back into a right relationship with him and others.

THE UNEXPECTED

We see Christ's loving patience on display when he responds to the expert in religious law, not with condemnation, but with a story that would nudge him to a more complete understanding of what it meant to love his neighbor as himself (kind of a *yada yada* moment).

Now if you have been around the church for any length of time you have heard the story of "The Good Samaritan." We all know the basic moral of the story: actions show love. While this is true, I believe there may be more to this story. So, let's fight "change blindness" and look at this story with fresh eyes.

"A Jewish man was traveling on a trip from Jerusalem to Jericho, and he was attacked by bandits. They stripped him of his clothes, beat him up, and left him half dead beside the road.[97]

Ok, here we have a Jewish man, a guy who is on the same team as Jesus' immediate target audience; and, to add to his "cultural currency," he was coming from the most holy city, Jerusalem. So, the picture Jesus is painting for his listener is that of a devout Jewish male, someone fellow Jews would find most natural and culturally encouraged to love.
But check out what happens next:

"By chance a priest came along. But when he saw the man lying there, he crossed to the other side of the road and passed him by.[98]

Let's be honest, there are some people who you do not expect to help anyone: aluminum siding salesmen, IRS agents, and Las Vegas pit bosses. But a priest? Certainly a priest would help someone, especially if that someone was on the same team. But, no, he crossed to the other side. This is the cultural equivalent of the pastor of your church seeing you

---

[97] Luke 10:30 (NLT)

[98] Luke 10:31 (NLT)

beat up and playing the "Oh, I did not see you at the market. . ." routine.

> "A Temple assistant walked over and looked at him lying there, but he also passed by on the other side.[99]

The next candidate, the Temple assistant, is someone who actually works for a living. He's *one of the people*; surely he will help. It is one thing for the pastor/priest to walk on by, but not the church secretary; they are always so nice. . . Unfortunately, strike two.

> "Then a despised Samaritan came along, and when he saw the man, he felt compassion for him. Going over to him, the Samaritan soothed his wounds with olive oil and wine and bandaged them. Then he put the man on his own donkey and took him to an inn, where he took care of him.[100]

Here is where the story gets good. Here we have the aluminum siding salesman, IRS agent, or Vegas pit boss (take your pick) come by and actually help this poor guy, a man from the far end of the social spectrum.

---

[99] Luke 10:32 (NLT)

[100] Luke 10:33-34 (NLT)

"The next day he handed the innkeeper two silver coins, telling him, 'Take care of this man. If his bill runs higher than this, I'll pay you the next time I'm here."[101]

I think this is the most inspiring and challenging part of this story. Not only did the Samaritan help him in his immediate need, but he also made a long term commitment to his restoration. As Christians I think we have become very good at short term, feel good, love of our neighbor. But, here we are shown that loving your neighbor is not a short term, one shot deal. True Christ-like love is a long-term commitment to restoration and healing.

"Now which of these three would you say was a neighbor to the man who was attacked by bandits?" Jesus asked.

The man replied, "The one who showed him mercy."

Then Jesus said, "Yes, now go and do the same."[102]

"Now go and do the same." As much as I would like to manage the expectation to love my

---

[101] Luke 10:35 (NLT)

[102] Luke 10: 36-37 (NLT)

neighbor as myself, I keep being confronted with the question, what if Jesus really meant it?

THE GOOD NIGERIAN

In the spring of 2009 I had the opportunity to go to Benin, Africa to meet with different organizations that were fighting child trafficking in the western region of the continent. After traveling from Tallahassee, Florida to Atlanta, spending the night in Germany, and finally arriving the next day in Nigeria (wearing the same clothes I left with), I was expecting to be picked up by a representative of one of the groups (Unseen Stories), to drive the final 60 miles to Couteneu, Benin.

But there was a hang up. I had some problems at immigration and they decided to deny my Visa, blocking me from entering Nigeria. I was taken into a small room with concrete floors and told to sit in there with several other unfortunates who had also ended up on the opposite end of a Nigerian welcome.

For the next 4 hours, without food, water or access to a bathroom we all sat in a ventilation-free room watching bugs crawl in and out of the cracks.

Around midnight a man in a uniform informed me that I would be sleeping in the airport that night, but I would be able to fly out the next day at 6:25pm to Benin. When I asked him if I could get a 24 hour Visa and stay in a hotel, he laughed. "Follow me to your accommodations," he said, with a hint of irony that even I, in my travel-weary state could detect.

After walking for a few minutes he pointed to the floor in the airport lobby and said, "You can sleep here."

As he walked away with my passport, I cried out to God in my sleepless funk, "God, I am tired, thirsty, hungry, and I miss my family. I am sure you are doing something here, but how about throwing me a bone?"

While I was praying I was surveying where I was going to sleep and saw a Delta airport lounge with one light on. I thought to myself, "I am a Delta Sky Miles member, maybe I can buy a day pass."

I ran up to the Delta lounge, but before I could even enter the young lady at the counter cleaning up informed me that they were closed for the evening. I told her I was a Delta Sky Miles member and asked what time they were open tomorrow – and if I could buy a day pass? She politely replied, "They no longer serve Delta members and they did not sell day passes."

My hopes dashed, I thanked her and turned for the door, resigned to my fate of no food, water, or a bed. As I turned to walk out she said, "Wait. Would you like something to eat and drink before you go?" Before I knew it she produced some water and sandwiches. As I poured water into my dehydrated shell, she said, "I am going to put down some newspaper on the floor and try to find a blanket so you do not have to sleep in the terminal. You can sleep here tonight."

I couldn't believe my ears. I told her, "You are an angel." (She probably just took it as a figure of speech, but at the moment I meant it literally.) She smiled and handed me a piece of paper with an internet password on it.

I couldn't believe it! I prayed to God that I was hungry, thirsty, tired and missed my family and He fed me, gave me water, a safe place to lay my head, and now internet so I could Skype my family. This was far beyond my weary (managed) expectations.

The *coup de grace* to my increasingly humbled faith came as I booted up my computer to Skype my family. She offered me a cup of coffee. I thought, "Are you kidding me?" I didn't even ask for that! As I sat down to drink my coffee and talk with my family, I thanked God for all the blessings He had shown me.

PRAYING WITH ADE

The next morning, Ade (the angel God sent me) woke me up and handed me a toiletry kit and said there was a shower I could use in the next room. (Free advice: If someone in a third world country suggests that you take a shower, you probably need it.)

After showering and reflecting on the power of water to restore and reinvigorate, I walked out and noticed Ade was reading a Bible.

I sat down and dropped the P-Bomb (told her that I was a pastor). She opened up and started to tell me her story of how she was raised Muslim and had converted to Christianity. As we talked her eyes grew moist as she recounted her life of broken dreams. I felt a peace in my heart saying, "This is why I have you here." I looked at her and asked if I could pray for her. She said, "Please."

This experience in Nigeria put me in need for someone to love me as herself. Ade, could have lost her job if they found out what she had done for me,

192

but she helped my anyway. I will never forget what she did for me and I hope that it will make me more aware of those who need a Good Samaritan.

chapter sixteen
Tangible Hand of Christ

"The impersonal hand of government can never replace the helping hand of a neighbor."
-Hubert H. Humphrey (1911 - 1978)

One of my favorite illustrations by Dwight L. Moody is about an encounter he had with a painting early on in his ministry. The story goes that one day he saw a painting of a woman on a small boat in the middle of a raging storm clinging to the mass of the ship which was illustrated as the cross. As he looked at the picture he thought to himself, "Now that is the picture of Christianity."

Many years later he encountered a different painting by the same artist, of the same woman, in the same boat, and still in the middle of a raging storm clinging to the cross-like mass. The only difference this time, she had only one hand on the cross while the other reached out to help someone into the boat. He thought to himself, "Now that is the true picture of Christianity."

194

There is no substitute for the hand of someone who is committed to you living out the life God has envisioned for you. At our church we have an axiom: money is attached to a hand. What this means is when we give, there is a relational commitment to what we are giving toward; much like the Good Samaritan coming back to assure the restoration of the Jewish man he rescued.

While giving money to a cause is good, giving your money and hand is even better. It is a lot harder to get relationally involved. I think that is why so many of us gravitate toward "drive by humanitarianism."

Drive by humanitarianism may cost you some resources, but it does not require you to get your hands dirty. It is a way for us to manage God's command to love others in a way that does not expose us relationally. When you are relationally connected to a cause, person, or church you can be hurt – and for most of us, that is too large a risk to take in our already more than complicated lives. After all, doesn't the government take care of the hurting in our society?

SEPARATION OF STATE AND CHURCH

I find it interesting that whenever there is a prayer at a school function, some atheist will cause a stink about separation of church and state. I find it interesting on several levels.

First, as far as I am concerned, if a group of people wanted to talk to an imaginary friend in the sky (atheist view of God), I think I would just have pity on them for how confused they are. I would not insist on legislating them into silence. Second, if anyone is encroaching on someone else's turf, it is the government.

Taking care of orphans, widows, and the under-resourced in our communities is the responsibility of the church. It is one of the things we have been called to do. Unfortunately, the church has often abdicated its responsibility to the state. It has gone so far that even people who are part of the church now think that caring for the "least of these" is the responsibility of the state.[103]

I have a dear friend who works for the State in social services. We have had many discussions about this, but the mutual conclusion we have reached is that the State does because the Church didn't.

One day I tried to paint a picture for him of what I would love to see happen. I told him that I wish the church was so faithful to the "least of these" that when a politician came up with a new social program to care for people, people would just scratch their heads in confusion and ask, "Why would we do that? The church does that and does a great job at it. There is no way the government could do it any better."

This is not supposed to be a commentary on the role of government; it is an indictment of the church's failure to fulfill the call to be an advocate for

---

[103] Matthew 25:40 (NLT) [40] "And the King will say, 'I tell you the truth, when you did it to one of the least of these my brothers and sisters, you were doing it to me!'

justice and an instrument of hope.[104] As a pastor I understand how hard it is to balance the needs of the church with the needs of the under-resourced in our communities, country, and world. Where do you start? What do you do?

ENTRUSTED AND TRUSTING

I think the answer may be right in front of you. Many times we can become paralyzed by the overwhelming need that is in our communities, country, and world. I remember one particular morning my wife and I were having breakfast at El Patio in Panajachel, Guatemala (if you are ever there get the plato de fruta grande).

The day before was pretty busy visiting some homes our church helped build and speaking at a pretty enthusiastic church that went pretty late. So, we were happy to be leisurely enjoying our café, plato de fruta grandes, and panqueques that morning when we felt a tug on our table. When we looked at the source of the tug our eyes saw a young, boy in ragged clothing pointing at our half-eaten panqueques.

We both felt some shame for our kingly breakfast as we gave the little boy our left over

---

[104] Isaiah 51:5 (NLT) 5 "My mercy and justice are coming soon. My salvation is on the way. My strong arm will bring justice to the nations. All distant lands will look to me and wait in hope for my powerful arm."

panqueques. He disappeared as quickly as he had shown up. It could not have been 60 seconds before he reappeared with twenty of his closest friends, all looking in need of a meal as their friend did only minutes before.

What is a follower of Christ to do? We can't feed and take care of all these children until they are old enough to care for themselves. But we can do something.

One great thing about being a child of God is that you know your Dad loves people more than you ever could. You can rest assured that if you take care of those He entrusted to you He will give passion and resources to someone else to care for those entrusted to them. God loves people more than you ever can, and He is more faithful than we could ever be. Take care of what he has entrusted to you; make sure that others are better off because you are in their life, and allow God to take care of the rest.

MAKING PEOPLE BETTER

This is the prayer I pray every morning with my kids on the way to school. I pray that they will make people better than if they were not there. I do this because I want them to realize that their actions and attitudes can have a direct impact on the success, health, and happiness of others.

I heard a sports commentator state once that the reason Michael Jordan was such a great player is that he made everyone around him better. The Bulls were a good team without Michael, but something happened when he was on the court; they became a great team, a legacy. There was something about him that made everyone better and that was what made him so great.

Part of this, I'm sure was just natural ability, but I also believe that he intentionally inspired those around him to play better with him on the floor. Loving others can be tending to their physical needs, but it is also helping them live out the life God has envisioned for them.

One of my favorite scriptures, illustrating loving others through inspiration is found in Hebrews 10:24 (NLT), "Think of ways to encourage one another to outbursts of love and good deeds."

I love the imagery the writer of Hebrews uses here. The picture of premeditated inspiration that results in someone bursting out of their stagnation and uncontrollably spreading love and good deeds all around them. But, if we're honest, we have to recognize that it can be tough to get as close to people as Jesus modeled for us and ultimately called us to. The potential of being hurt so often holds us back.

THE BARK IS WORSE THAN THE BITE?

I have been traveling a lot more than I care to as of late. Hotels, living out of a backpack, and munching overly processed food is not my idea of a long term recipe for a healthy life. One thing that I do enjoy about traveling, however, is being able to run in new environments. It acquaints me with new locales and communities, and gives me space to think.

One morning while I was running in Atlanta, I ran past several homes with dogs. Not an unusual experience for a runner to encounter dogs, but this morning these encounters spurred my thinking to ponder the different people in my life.

I encountered one particular dog that started viciously barking at me as I approached. It was as if he was yelling, "Come one step closer and I'll rip your face off!" Luckily he was behind a fence, so his scare tactics struck me as more humorous than threatening.

As I continued down the road, at a truly uninspiring pace, I came across another dog. It ran up to me with a wagging tale, unreasonably excited I was there. She happily bounced along with me the length of her yard and seemed genuinely sad that I continued down the road without her.

Finally, I came across a dog that, much like the second one, came and greeted me with wagging tale and welcoming spirit. As I ran down the sidewalk in front of his house, he too bounced along encouraging me at every step. When we got to the end of his yard fence and I continued running down the street, his demeanor changed from happy and welcoming to ferocious and threatening.

As I continued down the road, listening to the dog bark his lungs out, I began thinking about the three different dogs that I had encountered during my run. There was one that was very up front about his lack of appreciation for my presence, another which was very excited about my time with her, and finally there was one that acted one way to my face and quite differently when I turned my back.

We've all encountered these three types. We have those in our life who are against us from the get go and they make no bones about their position. Then there are those who are always happy to see us, and can't wait till we run by again. Those two types of people are a blessing in our life; you know where you stand with them, whether they are or are not going to support you when you are not there.

However, the most dangerous type of person is the final type, the one whose demeanor changes drastically when you've gone. We have all had people in our lives like this and it can be very damaging. It can make you question all your relationships, to doubt the loyalty of those who might prove to be true friends.

So, what is the healthy way to deal with the two-faced dog?

As hard as it may be, the healthy way to deal with the two faced dog is head on. In Matthew 18, Jesus says that if someone wrongs you that you are to go to them privately and point out their offence. This can be really difficult. It is much easier to go and complain about the person to someone else, but by doing so we become the same as them. Jesus has called you to living out a higher calling and to love other as you love yourself.

SOCIAL EXCELLENCE

*"So whether you eat or drink, or whatever
you do, do it all for the glory of God."*
-Apostle Paul[105]

Social Excellence comes down to loving others as you love yourself. This usually falls into one of two categories: people you know and people you don't know.

People You Know: Cherishing every conversation as a priceless gift, being shared between two people who Christ loves. Am I saying that a conversation about the weather is important? Yes.

One secret we have lost in the ever increasing speed of our world – something the ancients knew and cherished – is that every conversation is important. I often have to remind myself of this fact. I find myself drifting easily when someone is telling me a lengthy story, or giving a detailed explanation about something they are interested in. I have to remind myself that, even though on the surface it may not be particularly compelling to me, this person matters, and that they are sharing something about themselves. That is always important.

The very fact that they are opening up themselves to me, reaching out and making a connection, letting me know that I am important to them, and confirming that I am not alone in this

---

[105] 1 Corinthians 10:31 (NLT)

isolated, go-go world is the most important conversation you can have.

People You Don't Know: Loving people you don't know in a lot of ways can be easier than loving the people you know. Sometimes it is easier for us to see a picture of a starving child in a far off land and send some money than it is to walk across the street and help our elderly neighbor. It is easier because we know that child will never knock on our door and expect an emotional investment. Your elderly neighbor, though, very well might want you to come visit tomorrow afternoon.

Societal excellence is doing for others, not as you would have them do unto you, but as you would do for yourself.

"Excellence is a gift; be generous."

Group Swim

reach and pull

Group Swim
Section 6
Loving Others

Jump In:

(You can't swim unless you are in the water. The "Jump In" is an "ice breaker" question to get the group talking.)

When was a time in your life that another's love helped you move forward in your life?

Drill Set:

(Drills in swimming are used to improve speed and efficiency. Studying scripture in the same way refines the heart, soul, and mind to help us live out the vision God has for our life.)

Read: Matthew 25:31–46

How hard do you think it would be to separate sheep from goats?

What are the ways you can tell the difference between a sheep and a goat?

How hard is it for Jesus to separate followers of Him from people who do not follow Him?

According to Jesus in this scripture, what are the difference between His followers and those who did not follow Him?

Why do you think the "righteous ones" did not know they had served Jesus?

Is it possible that there is a connection between the ease of identifying a sheep because of their actives and identifying a follower of Christ because of their actions?

Do you think sheep have to force themselves to do sheep activities?

Do the activities of your life identify you as a follower of Christ?

According in verse 46, what is the reward for of being the tangible hand of Christ?

How do you reconcile Matthew 25:46 and Romans 3:21–26?

Do you lean toward works of faith?

How do you respond to; Saved by grace, saved for works?

Open Water Swim:

(An open water swim is the real deal, no walls to hold onto, plastic lane lines to keep people from bumping into you, or black lines painted on the bottom to keep you going in the right direction. This section is a suggestion for the participants in your group to go out and put into practice the scripture that was studied.)

Put into practice being the tangible hand of Christ.

part 7
SWIM TO WIN
putting it all together

chapter seventeen
ONE MORE STROKE

"Just keep swimming!"
-Dory (Finding Nemo)

No matter how athletic you are, you can't swim from Alcatraz Island to San Francisco in a single stroke, kick, and breath. It is a process. In fact there is only one determining factor that separates those who complete a race and those who do not.

The factor?

Those who continue to find it within themselves to take one more stroke, kick, and breath toward the finish line are the ones who succeed.

Every swimmer experiences pain and obstacles on their way to the finish line, but those who overcome are the ones who achieve the prize of completion. Swimming a lap in a pool or swimming around Manhattan Island (yes, people really do that), is the same for every swimmer, whether they swim fast or slow. Every swimmer needs to conjure up the courage to take one more stroke, kick, and breath toward the line until they reach the shore.

The same is true in life. Far too often we never pursue God's vision for our life because it seems too far away. We stare out at the water stretching out before us and say to ourselves, "I can't swim to the shore." That's the lie we tell ourselves. All too many of us never try. The truth is if you can take one stroke, you *can* go the distance.

I have coached people who want to start loving God with all their heart, soul, mind, and strength, who don't have the time or the energy to experience the life that they believe God has envisioned for them.

For example I was speaking with a mom in her mid-thirties who believed God was calling her to get her nursing degree so she could go on global outreach trips and help people. Her reason for not pursuing this dream was that she did not have the time or money to go to school full time.

A valid reason not to move forward, but I felt I had the relational right to speak into her life, so I asked,

"You know what they eventually call someone who takes one class at a time?"

"What?" She responded.

I replied, "A nurse."

This advice is particularly applicable to me lately. I am currently working on earning my doctorate and every day I seem to wake up to more obstacles. Regardless of the barriers, the question is always the same: Can I take one more stroke, kick, and breath toward the vision God has for my life?

The truth is that nothing worthwhile can be achieved in one fell swoop. It takes time, planning, and persistence. Everyone must continue to move toward God's vision for their life; when they reach it, they will be able to look back and realize that the journey was as important as the destination.

So, what is your race? What has God envisioned for you long ago? What is He beckoning you to move toward in order to make it a reality? Whatever race you are running – whether in business, school, or athletics – you don't need to finish the race today, you just need to take one more stroke, kick, and breath toward the shore.

WHAT DO YOU WANT TO BE GOOD AT?

A couple of years ago I commented to a training partner (who is faster than me) that I wanted to become a faster runner. "Don't you know the secret of becoming a faster runner?" he asked. When I told him no, he said simply, "If you want to become a faster runner, what you need to do is RUN."

Not really what I wanted to hear, but over the years I have taken this simple advice – and have become a much stronger and faster runner on account of it.

The other day I was in the gym talking to a trainer friend of mine while watching a guy banging out pull-ups like he was eating M&Ms. Shaking my head I told my trainer friend that I have never been able to crank out many pull-ups. He asked me, "Don't you know the secret to doing pull-ups?" *This sounds familiar*, I thought. "If you want to be able to do a lot of pull-ups," he said, "what you need to do is PULL-UPS."

This is what Margaret Feinberg calls a, "Sacred Echo," a truth heard from multiple unrelated sources.

I was thinking about this idea of having to practice the thing that you want to become good at and how it relates to living out a healthy integrated life. The question is simple. Do you want to experience the rich and satisfying life God has envisioned for you? Then practice living a healthy integrated life as often as possible.

Even though we want the secret shortcut to doing this life well, the reality is that it takes time, focus, and desire to become good at living a healthy integrated life.

LIFE BUDGET

For most of us the very mention of a budget brings up thoughts of settling for less than you want or a restrictive lifestyle. The reality is that a budget is freeing; a budget allows us to do more of the things we truly want to do. How so?

Let's say that you always dreamed of vacationing in Europe, but never seem to have the money to make it happen. The reality for most of us is that we have the money to do the things we truly want to do, we just spend it on other things without really thinking about it. For example say that a trip to Europe is going to cost around $2,000US. That is a lot of money.

What if I told you that you could be drinking a cappuccino in Italy this time next year without going into debt? The trick is making a decision on what you value the most. Research shows that the average weekday lunches out costs around $9 (tip, tax and drink). If you value drinking a cappuccino in Italy more than eating at a forgettable generic food joint five days a week for one year, you could save that $2,000US ($9 a day vs. $1 a day if you brown bagged it) and be drinking that cappuccino in Italy. Your values, your choice.

Like a financial budget a life budget helps you live out your dreams and values. Are you ok with living an ordinary life? Or do you want more? Are you tired of living a life of stress and lack of purpose? Do you want the life God has envisioned for you?

Experiencing this rich and satisfying life requires you to make daily choices that reflect your life values. In order to do this you need to make a life budget.

A life budget, like a financial budget, is based on your resources. Unlike a financial budget, however, in a life budget we all have total equality in our time resources. It does not matter if you are Bill Gates or a homeless person, you have the same amount of hours each day, week, month and year.

So, how are you going to invest the time you have been entrusted with in this life?

As we have discussed in this book, Jesus said the most important thing in life is to love God with all your heart, soul, mind, and strength, and loving others as yourself. I would say that this is a great place to start when setting up a life budget.

Let's call this life budget W.H.O.L.E. These are the things that you have to incorporate into every day if you want to experience the life God has envisioned for you.

W.H.O.L.E. Day		
W	Worship	Spirit/Spiritual Health
H	Heart	Heart/Emotional Health
O	Others	Loving others/Sociological Health
L	Learning	Mind/Intellectual Health
E	Eating and Exercise	Strength/Physical Health

W=Worship

Every day build your relationship with God. I know for many people the idea of building a relationship with God seems foreign; they don't even know where to start. It really isn't as foreign as you might think. God is the author of relationships. So, it stands to reason that the same rules that apply with your earthly relationships apply to your relationship with God.

Simply put, whatever you do to build a healthy relationship with a person do the same with God.

Spend time with God. Talk to God. Give to God. Receive from God. Be a part of what God is doing and make Him a part of your life.

H=Heart

Every day take care of your emotional wellbeing. Take time to rest and reflect on your day and your relationships. Make sure you have a right relationship with God and people.

O=Others

Something amazing happens to us when we serve others. When we give of our time, talents, and treasures to lift someone up, we are tapping into the very nature of God.[106] In order to experience a WHOLE day, love someone, not out of convenience or with hope of reciprocation, but sacrificially with the sole desire to make someone's circumstance better.

Remember you are the conduit of God's love and mercy, called to be the tangible hand of Christ in this lost and hurting world.

---

[106] Mark 10:45 "For even the Son of Man came not to be served but to serve others and to give his life as a ransom for many."

L=Learning

As most of us learned in school, scientists say that humans use only about 10 percent of their brain. This has been the premise for many sci-fi stories and Christian jokes. One day I was visiting a friend's church and I a man told me that he feels like he needs to leave his brain in the car when he goes to his church.

God gave you a brain, filled with curiosity. Don't be afraid to explore and learn. All truth is God's truth and He is big enough to handle any question you may come up with. So crack those books and stimulate your brain. Who knows, you may be the first person to use 11% of your brain.

E=Eating and Exercise

Food is the fuel for activity; activity needs fuel. Keep this in balance and make it a priority every day. Is it fair that you can't eat whatever you want and sit around all day and look and feel great? Fair has nothing to do with it, it's just the reality of life. Your body is the temple for the Holy Spirit. Take care of it.

YOU ARE AT THE TURNING POINT

Knowing what to do is one thing; doing it is another. I want to leave you with one last thought. In ancient Greece there were four major sporting events; the Olympics Games, Panhellenic Games, Pythian Games, and Isthmian Games. These were major events for which people would rearrange their lives in order to watch them. Unlike the modern day Olympic Games, the Isthmian Games were open to any free persons who wanted to participate, as long as they would submit themselves to 10 months of rigorous training and strict dietary regulation.

The Isthmian Games featured wrestling, boxing, chariot racing, but the pinnacle of the games was the foot race. The stadium itself was built at the bottom of a hill side on the isthmus in Corinth (hence the name). It has been estimated that as many as 100,000 people could have attended an event. The oval track was approximately 606 feet from end to end (about the size of two football fields), and in the center of the track were three columns with inscriptions on them.

Inscribed on the first column was the word, "Excel," reminding runners to get up to speed. On the next column was inscribed the word, "Hasten," encouraging runners to continue to move with purpose and speed. And the third column was inscribed with the word, "Turn," marking the single turn at the halfway point.

I believe the Apostle Paul was a sports fan. He often used sports imagery to communicate a deeper spiritual point (sound familiar?). In 1 Corinthians 9:24 he used the Isthmian running race as a compelling vision for a follower of Christ.[107]

---

[107] 1 Corinthians 9:24–27 (NLT) "24 Don't you realize that in a race everyone runs, but only one person gets the prize? So run to win! 25 All athletes are disciplined in their training. They do it to win a prize that will fade away, but we do it for an eternal prize. 26 So I run with purpose in every step. I am not just shadowboxing. 27 I discipline my body like an athlete, training it to do what it should. Otherwise, I fear that after preaching to others I myself might be disqualified."

I have so many pastor friends and peers who tell their congregations to invite an "unchurched" friend to church. As if getting someone who is "unchurched" to be "churched" is the goal.

Now I am not against the local church; I have given my life to being part of the local church. I believe the local church is the only entity on earth ordained by God to encourage, equip, and edify people in every aspect of their life, heart, soul, mind, strength, and relationships with others.

But, I am also keenly aware that getting someone to attend church is not the finish line; it is meant to be the *turning* point. This is illustrated by our church's purpose statement to Make, Mature, and Mobilize fully devoted followers of Christ.

In the context of Paul's racing illustration the first column would read, "Make": becoming a follower of Christ. This is the "excel" part of our faith journey, where we get up to speed. The next column would read, "Mature": maturing our faith in Jesus. This is the "hasten" part of our faith journey, where we continue to make progress toward living out the life God has envisioned for us. The third column would read, "Mobilize": it is time to "turn" from immaturity and start living a life that contributes to others' journeys. This is the point where we stop *going* to church and start *being* the Church, the physical manifestation of Jesus Christ in this lost and hurting world.

The really incredible thing is how different the course looks after the turn. As you head toward the true finish line you see the same columns on your way back, but now they take on a completely different meaning.

We read the column inscribed "Hasten"; now it means hasten our purpose of encouraging and equipping others in their faith journey. When we reach the final column, "Excel" now signifies that we are almost there – that we should push with all our might and finish well so we might receive the prize. What is that prize? To stand before you Creator and hear the words, "Well done, my good and faithful servant."

Group Swim

A life immersed

Group Swim
Section 7:
A Live Immersed

Jump In:

(You can't swim unless you are in the water. The "Jump In" is an "ice breaker" question to get the group talking.)

Do you believe you are experiencing the life God has envisioned for you?

Why or why not?

Drill Set:

(Drills in swimming are used to improve speed and efficiency. Studying scripture in the same way refines the heart, soul, and mind to help us live out the vision God has for our life.)

Read: 1 Corinthians 9:24–27 and John 10:10

What does running to win mean?

Do you believe Jesus has envisioned a rich and satisfying life for you?

What is a biblical definition of a rich and satisfying life?

What does disciplined in training mean in the context of a follower of Christ?

What is the eternal prize for a follower of Christ?

Read: Mark 12:28-31 and Matthew 28:18–20

In Matthew 28, Jesus instructs His disciples to teach other followers to obey all the commands He had given them?

Knowing that Jesus said, loving God with all your heart, soul, mind, strength, and loving other as yourself is the most important commandment, what should we focus on in life?

What impact could followers of Christ on their unbelieving friends if they were experiencing a rich and satisfying life?

Do you think there is a connection between the Great Commandment (Matthew 28:18-20), The Great Commission (Mark 12:28-31), and a rich and satisfying life (John 10:10)?

Open Water Swim:

(An open water swim is the real deal, no walls to hold onto, plastic lane lines to keep people from bumping into you, or black lines painted on the bottom to keep you going in the right direction. This section is a suggestion for the participants in your group to go out and put into practice the scripture that was studied.)

Make The Great Commandment the primary grid you make all your life decisions through.

Appendix 1
40-Days of Living a W.H.O.L.E. Life

This is a transformational 40-day life coaching experience which is designed as a practical application of *Immersion*. This life coaching experience will help you live out the vision God has for your life. Over the next 40-days this guide will coach you to implement loving God with all your heart, soul, mind, strength, and loving others as yourself into your daily W.H.O.L.E. life.

Please check with your physician before starting any diet and exercise program.

W.H.O.L.E Plan

- **Week One:**
    - Read part 1 of Immersion
    - Participate in a Group Swim study
    - Create your W.H.O.L.E. life budget (Appendix 3)
    - Fill in daily W.H.O.L.E. Worksheet (Appendix 4)
- **Week Two:**
    - Read part 2 of Immersion
    - Participate in a Group Swim study
    - Fill in daily W.H.O.L.E. Worksheet
- **Week Three:**
    - Read part 3 of Immersion
    - Participate in a Group Swim study
    - Fill in daily W.H.O.L.E. Worksheet
- **Week Four:**
    - Read part 4 of Immersion

- o Participate in a Group Swim study
- o Fill in daily W.H.O.L.E. Worksheet
- **Week Five:**
  - o Read part 5 of Immersion
  - o Participate in a Group Swim study
  - o Fill in daily W.H.O.L.E. Worksheet
- **Week Six:**
  - o Read part 6 of Immersion
  - o Participate in a Group Swim study
  - o Fill in daily W.H.O.L.E. Worksheet
- **Week Seven:**
  - o Read part 7 of Immersion
  - o Participate in a Group Swim study
  - o Fill in daily W.H.O.L.E. Worksheet

Jump into a W.H.O.L.E. Day

- Get acquainted with the Daily Habits
  - o See Examples (Appendix 2)
- Discover BMI or Body Fat Percentage
  (http://www.cdc.gov/healthyweight/assessing/bmi/)
- Discover Daily Energy/Calorie Needs
  (http://nutrition.about.com/od/changeyourdiet
  /a/calguide.htm)

W.H.O.L.E. Daily Habits

Worship/Spirit: (Start small and increase by 1 minute a week until you reach your Life Budget goal.)

- Read your Bible
- Pray
- Journal

Heart: Do activities that increase your emotional wellness.

Others: Do something (no matter how small) every day to make someone's life better.

Learning/Mind: Read every day or sign up for a class.

Eating: Eat food as close to the source as possible.

(Great recipes can be found at www.cookinglight.com)

Activity: (Start small and increase by 5 minutes a week until your reach your Life Budget goal.)

- 30 minutes of cardio a day
    - Walking
    - Running
    - Swimming
    - Cycling

Rest: In bed with lights, computer, and TV off for seven to eight hours.

Use the E.A.R. formula found on page 171 to listen to your body and discover a balanced plan.

Appendix 2

The Following are some Examples of W.H.O.L.E. Activities

Examples of Worship/Soul/Spirit Activities

- Attend a Worship Gathering
- Write a poem, song, or artistic expression of God's love.
- Go to a place in nature where you experience God then read and meditate on Psalm 139
- Go to a Bible study.
- Meditate on the Lord's Prayer
- Read all your journal entries you have written up this point.
- Invite some friends over and dinner. Get your menu from www.cookingwiththebible.com and do a Bible study based on the meal.
- **Ongoing:** Incorporate healthy spirit activities into your W.H.O.L.E. Living

Heart/Emotion

- Write down in the below column what you need forgiveness for and what your need to give forgiveness for.

Forgiveness List	
Need forgiveness for:	Need to give forgiveness for:

Now prioritize your forgiveness list according to the pain it has caused you.

Prioritized Your Forgiveness List	
Need forgiveness for:	Need to give forgiveness for:

- Identify obstacles to getting these items off your list.
- Get one NEED/GIVE forgiveness off your list
- Write and mail a letter to someone who has made an impact in your life.
- Share your list with someone you trust.
- **Ongoing:** Incorporate healthy emotional activities into your W.H.O.L.E. Living

Examples of Loving Others Activities

- Rest/Recovery
- Go out of your way to be courteous while driving today
- Make up a vegetable platter for your co-workers to snack on
- Walk around your neighborhood and pick up trash
- Go through your clothes and bring some good stuff to Goodwill
- Do something nice for someone on your street
- Go and serve for a few hours at a local charity
- **Ongoing:** Incorporate healthy physical activities into your W.H.O.L.E. Living

Examples of Learning/Mind/Intellect Activities

- Memorize Philippians 4:4-9
- Read 30 minutes
- Take a class or go back to school
- Learn a second language
- Lean a new skill
- **Ongoing:** Incorporate healthy learning activities into your W.H.O.L.E. Living

Examples of Eating and Exercise Activities

- Join a walking or running group
- Find some friends to cycle with once a week
- Join a swim group at your local public pool
- Join a gym
- Take a pilates class
- Join a support group to kick a bad habit
- **Ongoing:** Incorporate healthy physical activities into your W.H.O.L.E. Living

Mark's Example Eating Plan
(This is how I eat.)

- Breakfast: (Choose one)
  - Whole grain oatmeal
  - Vegetable egg scramble (Use a no calorie non-stick spray)
  - Fruit and granola
- Mid-morning snack
  - Piece of fresh fruit
- Lunch (Choose one)

- o Skinless chicken breast or fish, brown rice, vegetable
- o Turkey sandwich (no cheese or mayo) on whole grain bread
- o Leafy salad with olive oil based dressing on the side
- o Sushi
- o Broth based soup
- Afternoon snack
  - o Piece of fresh fruit
- Dinner (Choose three)
  - o Vegetables
  - o Leafy salad with olive oil based dressing on the side
  - o Crab stuffed avocado
  - o Fish, chicken breast or turkey breast
  - o Sushi
  - o Brown rice

Appendix 3
W.H.O.L.E. Life Budget

Appendix 3 and 4 worksheets are ways to plan out your week in order to make sure you are incorporating The Great Commandment into your everyday life and moving toward living out the life God has envisioned for you.

I have included sample worksheets that I have filled out in order to give you an example of how to use the forms.

You will notice that every form is based on the foundation of The Great Commandment expressed through the W.H.O.L.E. acronym.

Foundations:

W=Worship: Soul/Spiritual Health

H=Heart: Heart/Emotional Health

0=Others: Loving others/Sociological Health

L=Learning: Mind/Intellectual Health

E=Eating & Exercise: Strength/Physical Health

Mark's W.H.O.L.E. (Tuesday Example) Life Budget

As a pastor my schedule drastically changes from day to day. I have taken the time to schedule each day to make sure I have a W.H.O.L.E. day each and every day.

W.H.O.L.E. Life Budget.	
Worship	45 minutes
Heart	30 minutes
Others	30 minutes
Learning	2 hours
Exercise	45 minutes
Eating	90 minutes
Work (Including Travel/prep Time)	10 Hours
Rest/Sleep	7 Hours
Free Time	1 hour
Total	**24 hours**

- 6am and read my Bible and pray for 30 minutes.
- oatmeal for breakfast (325 Calories)
- work at 7:30am
- Banana at 10AM (125 Calories).
- Sushi and swim group (600 Calories and 45 min.)
- Apple at 3pm (50 Calories)
- Head home from working 6pm
- Dinner with family (1,400 calories)
- Read with family 60 minutes
- Bible study with family (15 minutes)
- Play catch with my son. (30 minutes)
- Put kids to bed and pray with them
- Work on dissertation (2 hours)
- Journal/write (30 minutes)
- Pray with wife (15 minutes)
- Sleep at 11PM

W.H.O.L.E. Life Budget.	
Worship	
Heart	
Others	
Learning	
Exercise	
Eating	
Work (Including Travel/prep Time)	
Rest/Sleep	
Free Time	
Total	24 hours

W.H.O.L.E. Life Budget.	
Worship	
Heart	
Others	
Learning	
Exercise	
Eating	
Work (Including Travel/prep Time)	
Rest/Sleep	
Free Time	
Total	24 hours

W.H.O.L.E. Life Budget.

Worship	
Heart	
Others	
Learning	
Exercise	
Eating	
Work (Including Travel/prep Time)	
Rest/Sleep	
Free Time	
Total	24 hours

W.H.O.L.E. Life Budget.	
Worship	
Heart	
Others	
Learning	
Exercise	
Eating	
Work (Including Travel/prep Time)	
Rest/Sleep	
Free Time	
Total	24 hours

W.H.O.L.E. Life Budget.	
Worship	
Heart	
Others	
Learning	
Exercise	
Eating	
Work (Including Travel/prep Time)	
Rest/Sleep	
Free Time	
Total	24 hours

W.H.O.L.E. Life Budget.	
Worship	
Heart	
Others	
Learning	
Exercise	
Eating	
Work (Including Travel/prep Time)	
Rest/Sleep	
Free Time	
Total	24 hours

W.H.O.L.E. Life Budget.

Worship	
Heart	
Others	
Learning	
Exercise	
Eating	
Work (Including Travel/prep Time)	
Rest/Sleep	
Free Time	
Total	24 hours

Appendix 4
SAMPLE: W.H.O.L.E. Worksheet

Week May 4th-11th	Sunday	Monday	Tuesday	Wednesday	Thursday	Friday	Saturday
Worship	Went to a worship gathering	Prayed 15 min. Read Bible 5 min. Journal 10 Min.	Prayed 15 min. Read Bible 5 min. Journal 10 Min.	Prayed 15 min. Read Bible 5 min. Journal 10 Min.	Prayed 15 min. Read Bible 5 min. Journal 10 Min.	Prayed 15 min. Read Bible 5 min. Journal 10 Min.	Prayed 15 min. Read Bible 5 min. Journal 10 Min.
Heart	Rest	Had coffee with a friend	Asked spouse about their dreams.	Wrote a letter of forgiveness	Painted a picture	Called an old friend	Spent time with friends
Others	Rest	Moved a shopping cart away from a car.	Volunteered 1 hour at shelter	Brought a bag and picked up trash on my walk.	Mowed my neighbor's lawn	Left open the best parking spot.	Delivered food with above.
Learning	Rest	Read 20 min.	Read 25 min.	Started learning a 2nd language	Signed up for a pottery class	Read 45 min.	Read and worked on my 2nd language
Eating & exercise	BMI 23.75	Walked 30 min. 2400 Cal.	Swam 35 min. 2500 Cal.	Walked 30 min. 2200 Cal.	Rode bike 45 min. 2350 Cal.	Walked 40 min. 2550 Cal.	Run/walk 40 min. 2400 Cal.

W.H.O.L.E. Worksheet

Week ___	Sunday	Monday	Tuesday	Wednesday	Thursday	Friday	Saturday
Worship							
Heart							
Others							
Learning							
Eating/ Exercise	BMI ___						

W.H.O.L.E. Worksheet

Week ___	Sunday	Monday	Tuesday	Wednesday	Thursday	Friday	Saturday
Worship							
Heart							
Others							
Learning							
Eating/ Exercise	BMI ___						

W.H.O.L.E. Worksheet

Week ___	Sunday	Monday	Tuesday	Wednesday	Thursday	Friday	Saturday
Worship							
Heart							
Others							
Learning							
Eating/ Exercise	BMI ___						

W.H.O.L.E. Worksheet

Week ___	Sunday	Monday	Tuesday	Wednesday	Thursday	Friday	Saturday
Worship							
Heart							
Others							
Learning							
Eating/ Exercise	BMI ___						

W.H.O.L.E. Worksheet

Week ___	Sunday	Monday	Tuesday	Wednesday	Thursday	Friday	Saturday
Worship							
Heart							
Others							
Learning							
Eating/ Exercise	BMI ___						

W.H.O.L.E. Worksheet

Week ___	Sunday	Monday	Tuesday	Wednesday	Thursday	Friday	Saturday
Worship							
Heart							
Others							
Learning							
Eating/ Exercise	BMI ___						

Appendix 5

Anxiety, Depression & Stress Symptoms

If you're concerned that you may be entering into an episode of stress depression and anxiety, you'll want to know the symptoms associated with these problems and how they affect sufferers. Here are the most common symptoms of stress, depression and anxiety:[108]

Lack of energy: This symptom is common to stress depression and anxiety and no matter how much you try, you just can't seem to get energized for anything. This affects motivation and so you're in a catch 22 situation. The less energetic you feel, the more your motivation levels drop. The less motivated you feel, the lower your energy levels become.

Exhaustion: This is major symptom of depression and it is so debilitating. This is a different kind of exhaustion than the exhaustion you feel say after strenuous physical exercise. In depression, the exhaustion is mentally and physically crushing. Even performing simple daily tasks is way too difficult and it doesn't matter how much you sleep, the exhaustion just won't go away.

Trembling Hands: This is mainly a stress or anxiety symptom. The sufferer may be in such a nervous,

[108] Concurring Stress: Get Your Life Back
http://www.conqueringstress.com/stress-symptom.html

fearful state that the body floods with powerful chemicals such as adrenaline. In this state, the brain is in a high status of alert and trembling hands are a noticeable, physical and uncontrollable symptom. Until of course, the root cause of it is addressed and the trembles will then disappear.

Disturbed Sleeping Patterns: This symptom is common to stress, depression and anxiety and it works in 2 main ways. The suffer will either sleep too much or more likely, will only sleep for a couple of hours a night, maybe even less. In many cases, sleep is disrupted because of vivid nightmares, which some sufferers may not even remember. Other sufferers have recurring nightmares. Although these vivid dreams may cause distress, please realize that it isn't representing anything about you, it is the stress, depression or anxiety that is causing the brain to work overtime and these vivid dreams are a symptom of this, so please don't blame yourself or feel guilty. The nightmares will disappear once stress, depression and anxiety are under control.

Excessive Worry: Mainly a symptom of anxiety and stress, excessive worry means the sufferer worries about even the smallest of life's events. A sufferer will be unable to find positive outcomes to anything and will continually assign negative outcomes to all situations. In continually assigning negative outcomes, life becomes very hard as sufferers are in a fearful state of mind for prolonged periods, a state that harms the body as well as the mind.

Irritable: Irritability is a major stress symptom as anyone who's been under severe stress (and most of us have at some point in our lives) will know this all too well. When you're under stress, you are stretched to your limit and your patience levels are thin. This explains why even the slightest thing can cause a sufferer to lose their temper or be off-handed or curt towards others. And even when the slightest mishap or accident occurs as they do so often during our daily routines, it will fuel the frustration causing more aggressive or nasty behavior. Again, this is a symptom of stress and the irritability goes away when stress is relieved.

Isolation: Wanting to shut out the world is another major symptom of depression, although stress sufferers can sometimes seek solitude too. Retreating into a solitary, lonely world further pushes the sufferer down the depression spiral – it's like self-imposed solitary confinement – making it even harder for sufferers to find a way out of depression. This is because sufferers feel uncomfortable or even awkward around others and would rather be alone to avoid this feeling.

Panic: This anxiety symptom arises because the sufferer is convinced a catastrophic outcome to an event - or a number of events - in life is imminent. Possible examples could include a wedding, a house move, a work situation, relationship issues, illness, flying, or speaking in public. Sufferers simply cannot change this focus and the more they think about this catastrophe, the more panic stricken they become. Fortunately, there are a number of ways to address this so a person doesn't enter the spiral that leads to panic.

Worthless Feelings: A symptom of depression although stress sufferers may also feel this way sometimes. This is a terrible feeling to have. Sufferers lose all sense of self-worth, self-esteem plummets and overly critical self-deprecation is performed, adding to the torment. Self-confidence erodes away to nothing and at this point, an individual will find no joy in life, including pastimes and activities that previously brought them so much joy and happiness. The good news is that confidence and self-esteem are skills that can be re-learned and along with many other skills form a crucial part in treating depression.

Guilt: A symptom common to stress, anxiety and depression, guilt can be a heavy burden for sufferers because it's a lose-lose situation: They will feel guilty about things they've done or they will feel guilty about things they didn't do. A continual replaying of events accompanied by regrets and "If only.." causes deep emotional anguish and heaps yet more torment on to an already tormented person. Guilt really is a powerful, destructive but ultimately worthless emotion yet the harm it inflicts on sufferers is immense. Guilt, like many other emotions, can be dealt with very effectively and this is another important skill to master in managing stress, depression and anxiety.

Headaches: Another common symptom of stress, depression and anxiety. This is a physical symptom and in some cases, the headaches turn into migraine, especially for people under severe stress. This is one symptom that shows problems like stress, depression and anxiety aren't "all in your mind" and clearly demonstrates how stress, depression and anxiety have physical as well as mental symptoms.

Muscle Pain: Mainly a symptom of depression but stress sufferers may also suffer muscle pain. Muscle pain symptoms will typically be backache and leg cramps. These symptoms can be so painful, and a problem is that sufferers will be unaware that the pain is a symptom of depression. Once the depression is controlled, the pain vanishes.

Racing Heartbeat: Not so common with depression, more a symptom of anxiety and stress. Again, the highly-aroused emotional state floods the body with adrenaline and the heart rate rises. This may also cause "butterflies" in the tummy as well.

Loss of Appetite: A symptom common to stress, anxiety and depression, loss of appetite is perhaps one of the most obvious consequences of stress, anxiety and depression because of the emotional state of the sufferer. No one feels like eating when they're frightened, panic stricken or feeling worthless and exhausted. There are some sufferers whose appetites have increased dramatically but they are in the minority. Loss of appetite is more common, and reducing food intake further affects energy levels and deprives the body of nourishment, further exacerbating stress, depression and anxiety. It's important to note that the causes of stress, depression and anxiety are not rooted in diet and diet alone cannot cure any of them. However, healthy eating does have a part to play, and it should be a part of your stress, anxiety and depression treatment.

Loss of Sex Drive: Just as above, this symptom occurs because of the emotional state of the sufferer. Paradoxically, many people who are depressed can seek emotional re-assurance from sex even though their sexual appetite has decreased. So loss of sex drive doesn't necessarily mean abstinence from sex. This is more common to depressed women than men, as for men, being in a highly stressed, anxious or depressed state can make the physical act of sex nigh-on impossible. For reasons that I hope are so obvious I need not go into any more detail! Again, as with the other symptoms, your sex drive will return once stress, depression and anxiety have been brought under control.

Appendix 6
Scripture Used in Immersion

Chapter 1

2 Timothy 4:7 (NLT) — 7 I have fought the good fight, I have finished the race, and I have remained faithful.

Mark 12:29–31 (NLT) — 29 Jesus replied, "The most important commandment is this: 'Listen, O Israel! The LORD our God is the one and only LORD.**30** And you must love the LORD your God with all your heart, all your soul, all your mind, and all your strength.'**31** The second is equally important: 'Love your neighbor as yourself.' No other commandment is greater than these."

Chapter 2

Psalm 37:23–24 (NLT) — 23 The LORD directs the steps of the godly. He delights in every detail of their lives. **24** Though they stumble, they will never fall, for the LORD holds them by the hand.

2 Corinthians 12:8 (NLT) — 8 Three different times I begged the Lord to take it away.

2 Corinthians 12:19 (NLT) — 19 Perhaps you think we're saying these things just to defend ourselves. No, we tell you this as Christ's servants, and with God as our witness. Everything we do, dear friends, is to strengthen you.

Chapter 3

John 5:6 (ESV) — 6 When Jesus saw him lying there and knew that he had already been there a long time, he said to him, "Do you want to be healed?"

John 5:6 (RSV) — 6 When Jesus saw him and knew that he had been lying there a long time, he said to him, "Do you want to be healed?"

Chapter 4

Ephesians 2:10 (NLT) — 10 For we are God's masterpiece. He has created us anew in Christ Jesus, so we can do the good things he planned for us long ago.

Proverbs 4:11 (NLT) — 11 I will teach you wisdom's ways and lead you in straight paths.

Hebrews 11:7, 8, 11, 21, 23, 31, & 32 (NLT) — 7 It was by faith that Noah built a large boat to save his family from the flood. He obeyed God, who warned him about things that had never happened before. By his faith Noah condemned the rest of the world, and he received the righteousness that comes by faith.

Hebrews 11:8 (NLT) — 8 It was by faith that Abraham obeyed when God called him to leave home and go to another land that God would give him as his inheritance. He went without knowing where he was going.

Hebrews 11:11 (NLT) — 11 It was by faith that even Sarah was able to have a child, though she was barren and was too old. She believed that God would keep his promise.

Hebrews 11:21 (NLT) — 21 It was by faith that Jacob, when he was old and dying, blessed each of Joseph's sons and bowed in worship as he leaned on his staff.

Hebrews 11:23 (NLT) — 23 It was by faith that Moses' parents hid him for three months when he was born. They saw that God had given them an unusual child, and they were not afraid to disobey the king's command.

Hebrews 11:31 (NLT) — 31 It was by faith that Rahab the prostitute was not destroyed with the people in her city who refused to obey God. For she had given a friendly welcome to the spies.

Hebrews 11:32 (NLT) — 32 How much more do I need to say? It would take too long to recount the stories of the faith of Gideon, Barak, Samson, Jephthah, David, Samuel, and all the prophets.

1 Corinthians 12:30 (NLT) — 30 Do we all have the gift of healing? Do we all have the ability to speak in unknown languages? Do we all have the ability to interpret unknown languages? Of course not!

2 Corinthians 12:7–9 (NLT) — 7 even though I have received such wonderful revelations from God. So to keep me from becoming proud, I was given a thorn in my flesh, a messenger from Satan to torment me and keep me from becoming proud. **8** Three different times I begged the Lord to take it away.**9** Each time he said, "My grace is all you need. My power works best in weakness." So now I am glad to boast about my weaknesses, so that the power of Christ can work through me.

Chapter 5

John 10:10 (NLT) — 10 The thief's purpose is to steal and kill and destroy. My purpose is to give them a rich and satisfying life.

Romans 3:23 (NLT) — 23 For everyone has sinned; we all fall short of God's glorious standard.

1 Corinthians 9:25–27 (NLT) — 25 All athletes are disciplined in their training. They do it to win a prize that will fade away, but we do it for an eternal prize.**26** So I run with purpose in every step. I am not just shadowboxing.**27** I discipline my body like an athlete, training it to do what it should. Otherwise, I fear that after preaching to others I myself might be disqualified.

1 Corinthians 13:12 (KJV 1900) — 12 For now we see through a glass, darkly; but then face to face: now I know in part; but then shall I know even as also I am known.

Philippians 3:13–14 (NLT) — 13 No, dear brothers and sisters, I have not achieved it, but I focus on this one thing: Forgetting the past and looking forward to what lies ahead,**14** I press on to reach the end of the race and receive the heavenly prize for which God, through Christ Jesus, is calling us.

Proverbs 3:6 (NLT) — 6 Seek his will in all you do, and he will show you which path to take.

2 Corinthians 8:7–15 (NLT) — 7 Since you excel in so many ways—in your faith, your gifted speakers, your knowledge, your enthusiasm, and your love from us—I want you to excel also in this gracious act of giving. **8** I am not commanding you to do this. But I am testing how genuine your love is by comparing it with the eagerness of the other churches. **9** You know the generous grace of our Lord Jesus Christ. Though he was rich, yet for your sakes he became poor, so that by his poverty he could make you rich. **10** Here is my advice: It would be good for you to finish what you started a year ago. Last year you were the first who wanted to give, and you were the first to begin doing it.**11** Now you should finish what you started. Let the eagerness you showed in the beginning be matched now by your giving. Give in proportion to what you have.**12** Whatever you give is acceptable if you give it eagerly. And give according to what you have, not what you don't have.**13** Of course, I don't mean your giving should make life easy for others and hard for yourselves. I only mean that there should be some equality.**14** Right now you have plenty and can help those who are in need. Later, they will have plenty and can share with you when you need it. In this way, things will be equal.**15** As the Scriptures say, "Those who gathered a lot had nothing left over, and those who gathered only a little had enough."

Chapter 6

1 Corinthians 1:27 (NLT) — 27 Instead, God chose things the world considers foolish in order to shame those who think they are wise. And he chose things that are powerless to shame those who are powerful.

Isaiah 55:9 (NLT) — 9 For just as the heavens are higher than the earth, so my ways are higher than your ways and my thoughts higher than your thoughts.

Philippians 4:12–13 (NLT) — 12 I know how to live on almost nothing or with everything. I have learned the secret of living in every situation, whether it is with a full stomach or empty, with plenty or little. **13** For I can do everything through Christ, who gives me strength.

Chapter 7

Matthew 14:29–30 (NLT) — 29 "Yes, come," Jesus said. So Peter went over the side of the boat and walked on the water toward Jesus. **30** But when he saw the strong wind and the waves, he was terrified and began to sink. "Save me, Lord!" he shouted.

Isaiah 41:10 (NLT) — 10 Don't be afraid, for I am with you. Don't be discouraged, for I am your God. I will strengthen you and help you. I will hold you up with my victorious right hand.

Chapter 8

Psalm 16:8 (NLT) — 8 I know the LORD is always with me. I will not be shaken, for he is right beside me.

1 Corinthians 10:31 (NLT) — 31 So whether you eat or drink, or whatever you do, do it all for the glory of God.

Chapter 9

Romans 6:23 (The Message) — 23 Work hard for sin your whole life and your pension is death. But God's gift is real life, eternal life, delivered by Jesus, our Master.

Genesis 2:7 (NLT) — 7 Then the LORD God formed the man from the dust of the ground. He breathed the breath of life into the man's nostrils, and the man became a living person.

Romans 3:27–28 (NLT) — 27 Can we boast, then, that we have done anything to be accepted by God? No, because our acquittal is not based on obeying the law. It is based on faith.**28** So we are made right with God through faith and not by obeying the law.

John 3:16–17 (NLT) — 16 "For God loved the world so much that he gave his one and only Son, so that everyone who believes in him will not perish but have eternal life.**17** God sent his Son into the world not to judge the world, but to save the world through him.

Chapter 10

Exodus 3:3 (NLT) — 3 "This is amazing," Moses said to himself. "Why isn't that bush burning up? I must go see it."

2 Timothy 3:16–17 (NIV84) — 16 All Scripture is God-breathed and is useful for teaching, rebuking, correcting and training in righteousness, **17** so that the man of God may be thoroughly equipped for every good work.

Philippians 4:6 (NLT) — 6 Don't worry about anything; instead, pray about everything. Tell God what you need, and thank him for all he has done.

1 Thessalonians 5:17 (ESV) — 17 pray without ceasing,

Matthew 6:7 (LEB) — 7 "But when you pray, do not babble repetitiously like the pagans, for they think that because of their many words they will be heard.

1 John 4:8 (NLT) — 8 But anyone who does not love does not know God, for God is love.

1 Chronicles 21:24 (NLT) — 24 But King David replied to Araunah, "No, I insist on buying it for the full price. I will not take what is yours and give it to the LORD. I will not present burnt offerings that have cost me nothing!"

Matthew 20:28 (NLT) — 28 For even the Son of Man came not to be served but to serve others and to give his life as a ransom for many."

Chapter 11

Matthew 7:14 (NLT) — 14 But the gateway to life is very narrow and the road is difficult, and only a few ever find it.

Genesis 1:26 (NLT) — 26 Then God said, "Let us make human beings in our image, to be like us. They will reign over the fish in the sea, the birds in the sky, the livestock, all the wild animals on the earth, and the small animals that scurry along the ground."

Exodus 3:6 (NLT) — 6 I am the God of your father—the God of Abraham, the God of Isaac, and the God of Jacob." When Moses heard this, he covered his face because he was afraid to look at God.

Chapter 12

2 Corinthians 5:17 (NLT) — 17 This means that anyone who belongs to Christ has become a new person. The old life is gone; a new life has begun!

Romans 7:6 (NLT) — 6 But now we have been released from the law, for we died to it and are no longer captive to its power. Now we can serve God, not in the old way of obeying the letter of the law, but in the new way of living in the Spirit.

1 Corinthians 6:20 (NLT) — 20 for God bought you with a high price. So you must honor God with your body.

Matthew 7:13–14 (NLT) — 13 "You can enter God's Kingdom only through the narrow gate. The highway to hell is broad, and its gate is wide for the many who choose that way.**14** But the gateway to life is very narrow and the road is difficult, and only a few ever find it.

Chapter 13

1 Corinthians 6:19–20 (NLT) — 19 Don't you realize that your body is the temple of the Holy Spirit, who lives in you and was given to you by God? You do not belong to yourself,**20** for God bought you with a high price. So you must honor God with your body.

Romans 12:2 (NLT) — 2 Don't copy the behavior and customs of this world, but let God transform you into a new person by changing the way you think. Then you will learn to know God's will for you, which is good and pleasing and perfect.

1 Corinthians 6:19–20 (NLT) — 19 Don't you realize that your body is the temple of the Holy Spirit, who lives in you and was given to you by God? You do not belong to yourself,**20** for God bought you with a high price. So you must honor God with your body.

1 Corinthians 10:31 (NLT) — 31 So whether you eat or drink, or whatever you do, do it all for the glory of God.

2 Corinthians 5:3 (NLT) — 3 For we will put on heavenly bodies; we will not be spirits without bodies.

Ezekiel 16:49 (NLT) — 49 Sodom's sins were pride, gluttony, and laziness, while the poor and needy suffered outside her door.

Philippians 1:10–11 (The Message) — 10 so that your love is sincere and intelligent, not sentimental gush. Live a lover's life, circumspect and exemplary, a life Jesus will be proud of: **11** bountiful in fruits from the soul, making Jesus Christ attractive to all, getting everyone involved in the glory and praise of God.

John 14:7 (NLT) — 7 If you had really known me, you would know who my Father is. From now on, you do know him and have seen him!"

John 14:9 (NLT) — 9 Jesus replied, "Have I been with you all this time, Philip, and yet you still don't know who I am? Anyone who has seen me has seen the Father! So why are you asking me to show him to you?

John 10:10 (NLT) — 10 The thief's purpose is to steal and kill and destroy. My purpose is to give them a rich and satisfying life.

Mark 7:6 (NLT) — 6 Jesus replied, "You hypocrites! Isaiah was right when he prophesied about you, for he wrote, 'These people honor me with their lips, but their hearts are far from me.

Matthew 8:16–17 (NLT) — 16 That evening many demon-possessed people were brought to Jesus. He cast out the evil spirits with a simple command, and he healed all the sick. **17** This fulfilled the word of the Lord through the prophet Isaiah, who said, "He took our sicknesses and removed our diseases."

Matthew 12:15 (NLT) — 15 But Jesus knew what they were planning. So he left that area, and many people followed him. He healed all the sick among them,

Matthew 15:30 (NLT) — 30 A vast crowd brought to him people who were lame, blind, crippled, those who couldn't speak, and many others. They laid them before Jesus, and he healed them all.

Mark 1:34 (NLT) — 34 So Jesus healed many people who were sick with various diseases, and he cast out many demons. But because the demons knew who he was, he did not allow them to speak.

Mark 3:10 (NLT) — 10 He had healed many people that day, so all the sick people eagerly pushed forward to touch him.

Mark 6:13 (NLT) — 13 And they cast out many demons and healed many sick people, anointing them with olive oil.

Matthew 8:4 (NLT) — 4 Then Jesus said to him, "Don't tell anyone about this. Instead, go to the priest and let him examine you. Take along the offering required in the law of Moses for those who have been healed of leprosy. This will be a public testimony that you have been cleansed."

Mark 1:44 (NLT) — 44 "Don't tell anyone about this. Instead, go to the priest and let him examine you. Take along the offering required in the law of Moses for those who have been healed of leprosy. This will be a public testimony that you have been cleansed."

Luke 5:14 (NLT) — 14 Then Jesus instructed him not to tell anyone what had happened. He said, "Go to the priest and let him examine you. Take along the offering required in the law of Moses for those who have been healed of leprosy. This will be a public testimony that you have been cleansed."

Chapter 14

1 Corinthians 6:18–20 (NLT) — 18 Run from sexual sin! No other sin so clearly affects the body as this one does. For sexual immorality is a sin against your own body.**19** Don't you realize that your body is the temple of the Holy Spirit, who lives in you and was given to you by God? You do not belong to yourself,**20** for God bought you with a high price. So you must honor God with your body.

1 Thessalonians 4:3–5 (NLT) — 3 God's will is for you to be holy, so stay away from all sexual sin.**4** Then each of you will control his own body and live in holiness and honor—**5** not in lustful passion like the pagans who do not know God and his ways.

Proverbs 23:2 (NLT) — 2 If you are a big eater, put a knife to your throat;

Ephesians 5:18 (NLT) — 18 Don't be drunk with wine, because that will ruin your life. Instead, be filled with the Holy Spirit,

1 Corinthians 11:21 (NLT) — 21 For some of you hurry to eat your own meal without sharing with others. As a result, some go hungry while others get drunk.

Chapter 15

Luke 10:25–37 (NLT) — 25 One day an expert in religious law stood up to test Jesus by asking him this question: "Teacher, what should I do to inherit eternal life?" **26** Jesus replied, "What does the law of Moses say? How do you read it?" **27** The man answered, " 'You must love the LORD your God with all your heart, all your soul, all your strength, and all your mind.' And, 'Love your neighbor as yourself.' " **28** "Right!" Jesus told him. "Do this and you will live!" **29** The man wanted to justify his actions, so he asked Jesus, "And who is my neighbor?" **30** Jesus replied with a story: "A Jewish man was traveling on a trip from Jerusalem to Jericho, and he was attacked by bandits. They stripped him of his clothes, beat him up, and left him half dead beside the road. **31** "By chance a priest came along. But when he saw the man lying there, he crossed to the other side of the road and passed him by.**32** A Temple assistant walked over and looked at him lying there, but he also passed by on the other side. **33** "Then a despised Samaritan came along, and when he saw the man, he felt compassion for him.**34** Going over to him, the Samaritan soothed his wounds with olive oil and wine and bandaged them. Then he put the man on his own donkey and took him to an inn, where he took care of him.**35** The next day he handed the innkeeper two silver coins, telling him, 'Take care of this man. If his bill runs higher than this, I'll pay you the next time I'm here.' **36** "Now which of these three would you say was a neighbor to the man who was attacked by bandits?" Jesus asked. **37** The man replied, "The one who showed him mercy." Then Jesus said, "Yes, now go and do the same."

Deuteronomy 6:5 (NLT) — 5 And you must love the LORD your God with all your heart, all your soul, and all your strength.

Luke 10:30–37 (NLT) — 30 Jesus replied with a story: "A Jewish man was traveling on a trip from Jerusalem to Jericho, and he was attacked by bandits. They stripped him of his clothes, beat him up, and left him half dead beside the road. **31** "By chance a priest came along. But when he saw the man lying there, he crossed to the other side of the road and passed him by.**32** A Temple assistant walked over and looked at him lying there, but he also passed by on the other side. **33** "Then a despised Samaritan came along, and when he saw the man, he felt compassion for him.**34** Going over to him, the Samaritan soothed his wounds with olive oil and wine and bandaged them. Then he put the man on his own donkey and took him to an inn, where he took care of him.**35** The next day he handed the innkeeper two silver coins, telling him, 'Take care of this man. If his bill runs higher than this, I'll pay you the next time I'm here.' **36** "Now which of these three would you say was a neighbor to the man who was attacked by bandits?" Jesus asked. **37** The man replied, "The one who showed him mercy." Then Jesus said, "Yes, now go and do the same."

Chapter 16

Matthew 25:40 (NLT) — 40 "And the King will say, 'I tell you the truth, when you did it to one of the least of these my brothers and sisters, you were doing it to me!'

Isaiah 51:5 (NLT) — 5 My mercy and justice are coming soon. My salvation is on the way. My strong arm will bring justice to the nations. All distant lands will look to me and wait in hope for my powerful arm.

1 Corinthians 10:31 (NLT) — 31 So whether you eat or drink, or whatever you do, do it all for the glory of God.

Chapter 17

Mark 10:45 (NLT) — 45 For even the Son of Man came not to be served but to serve others and to give his life as a ransom for many."

1 Corinthians 9:24–27 (NLT) — 24 Don't you realize that in a race everyone runs, but only one person gets the prize? So run to win!**25** All athletes are disciplined in their training. They do it to win a prize that will fade away, but we do it for an eternal prize.**26** So I run with purpose in every step. I am not just shadowboxing.**27** I discipline my body like an athlete, training it to do what it should. Otherwise, I fear that after preaching to others I myself might be disqualified.

VISIT
www.immersion4groups.com
Free downloads and content for your
small group, church, or support group.

16354401R00149

Made in the USA
Charleston, SC
16 December 2012